The Random House Book of
1001
Questions and Answers
About Planet Earth

Brian and Brenda Williams

Random House 🏠 **New York**

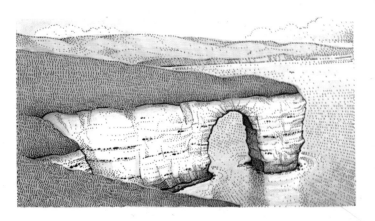

First American edition, 1993

Library of Congress Cataloging in Publication Data
Williams, Brian
   The Random House book of 1001 questions and
answers about planet earth / Brian and Brenda Williams.
   p. cm.
   Includes index.
   Summary: Curiosities and wonders about planet earth,
including its formation, history, physical features,
climate, volcanoes, earthquakes, deserts, ice caps,
pollution, oceans, atmosphere, vegetation, and resources.
1. Earth—Miscellanea—Juvenile literature.
[1. Earth—Miscellanea. 2. Questions and answers.]
I. Williams, Brenda. II. Title. III. Title: One thousand
and one questions and answers about planet earth.
IV. Title: 1001 questions and answers about planet earth.
V. Title: Book of 1001 questions and answers about planet
earth.
ISBN 0-679-83699-3 (pbk.)
QB631.4.W55 1993 92-15497 550-dc20

Manufactured in Spain 1 2 3 4 5 6 7 8 9 0

CONTENTS

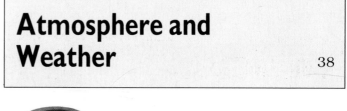

PLANET EARTH

What is a planet?

A planet is a world orbiting, or traveling around, a star. The Earth is a planet that orbits the Sun, a medium-sized star.

How many planets are there?

There are nine planets orbiting the Sun. They are Mercury (nearest the Sun), Venus, Earth, Mars, Jupiter, Saturn, Uranus, Neptune, and Pluto. In the night sky, the planets appear as tiny points of light, like stars.

Do other stars have planets?

There are millions and millions of stars in the Universe. Some probably have their own planets. Scientists think they have found at least one Earth-sized planet orbiting a distant star. The planet is 30,000 light-years away.

Which star is nearest to the Solar System?

Finding other planets in space is difficult because the stars are so distant. The nearest star to our Solar System, Proxima Centauri, is 4.3 light-years away. Light from it takes more than 4 years to reach the Earth!

What is earthshine?

Astronauts on the Moon saw the Earth apparently shining, just as we on Earth see the Moon bright in the night sky. This is earthshine. Stars shine by their own light, but planets shine only because they reflect a star's light. Planets are much smaller and cooler than stars.

Nine planets orbit the Sun. The largest are Jupiter and Saturn.

Pluto

Neptune

Uranus

Saturn

Mercury

Venus

Earth

Jupiter

Mars

Sun

Most scientists think the Universe began with a vast explosion of energy—the big bang. This sent matter flying through space. The matter came together to form galaxies of stars. Our Sun is a medium-sized star among hundreds of billions of stars in our galaxy, the Milky Way.

How was the Earth formed?

The Sun and its planets were formed at about the same time. A whirling cloud of gas and dust collected in space. It grew denser and denser as gravity squeezed the gas and dust together. Most of the cloud formed the Sun. What was left over became the planets.

How old is the Earth?

The Universe began to form over 15 billion years ago. The Earth is much younger. It is about 4.6 billion years old.

What are moons?

A moon is a small world going around a planet. It is held in orbit by the planet's gravity. All but 2 of the Sun's planets—Mercury and Venus—have moons. The Earth has only 1 moon, but Saturn seems to have at least 22.

Why is the Moon lifeless?

The Moon is only 2,160 miles in diameter. (It would just about cover Australia.) Its gravity is only one-sixth of the Earth's gravity, making it too weak to hold down the gases left in its atmosphere after it formed. They floated away into space, leaving the Moon a dead, airless world.

Is the Moon as old as the Earth?

Yes. The Moon came into being when the Sun and its planets were formed, about 4.6 billion years ago. At first, the Moon was a red-hot ball of molten rock. As it cooled, it hardened more rapidly than the Earth because it was smaller.

The Moon is cold and lifeless. It has no atmosphere, and its rocky surface is pitted with craters made by meteorites crashing into it.

How fast does the Moon spin?

The Moon rotates, or spins, once each time it goes around the Earth. That means it spins once every 29.25 days—the same time it takes to complete one orbit around the Earth.

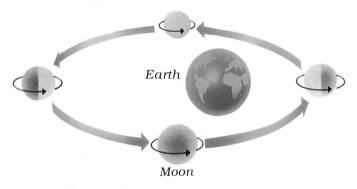

The Moon always shows the same side to us. We see the part of the Moon lit by the Sun.

Can we see all of the Moon?

One side of the Moon is always turned away from the Earth. As the newly formed Moon cooled, the Earth's gravity pulled at it. This slowed the Moon's spin and raised a bulge on the side nearest the Earth. Because the Moon rotates once as it orbits the Earth, this same side always faces us. Not until spacecraft flew around the Moon could we see what the far side was like.

How does the Moon affect the Earth?

The Moon's gravity affects us every day. The pull of the Moon causes the rise and fall of the ocean tides (see page 52). The Moon can also block out the Sun's light during an eclipse, casting a black shadow across part of the Earth.

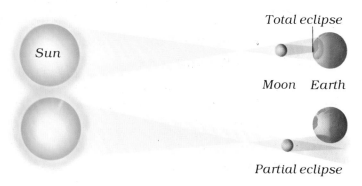

A solar eclipse occurs when the Moon passes between the Earth and the Sun.

How big is the Earth?

The Earth is the fifth largest of the Sun's family of planets. Its circumference (the distance around the Earth) is 24,902 miles. The Earth is dwarfed by the giant planet Jupiter, which is 318 times more massive. It is big enough to swallow all the other planets in the Sun's system.

Is the Earth putting on weight?

The Earth weighs about 6.6 sextillion tons. It is getting heavier each year because it is hit by meteorites—pieces of rock moving through space—which add to its weight.

Is the Earth really round?

The Earth is not a perfectly round sphere. It is slightly flattened at the poles. This flattening is caused by the speed of its spin.

A satellite image of the Earth

Where is the equator?

The equator is an imaginary line around the middle of the Earth. It is the line of 0° latitude. The fattest part of the Earth is actually just below the equator.

Where is the North Pole?

Near the middle of the Arctic Ocean. It is the northern point where all the lines of longitude meet.

Where are the Tropics?

The Tropics are regions of the Earth that lie within 1,600 miles north and 1,600 miles south of the equator. The Tropic of Cancer is 23° 27′ north of the equator. The Tropic of Capricorn is 23° 27′ south of the equator. Within the Tropics the Sun shines directly overhead.

What are the hemispheres?

A hemisphere is half of a globe. On maps and globes, the equator (0° latitude) divides the planet into two halves. These are the Northern and Southern hemispheres. An imaginary line around the Earth from the North Pole to the South Pole (the line of 0° longitude) divides the Eastern and Western hemispheres.

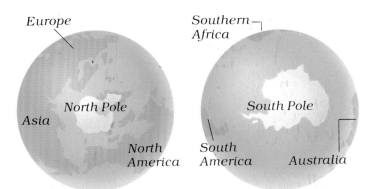

The Northern Hemisphere (left) includes most of Asia and all of North America and Europe. The Southern Hemisphere includes southern Africa, Australia, and most of South America.

How long and wide is the Earth?

From pole to pole the distance through the Earth measures 7,900 miles. Its diameter at the equator is 7,926 miles.

Why does the Earth orbit the Sun?

Like other planets in the Solar System, the Earth is held in an orbit, or path, as it travels around the Sun. It is held in place by the Sun's gravity.

How far away is the Sun?

The Earth is about 93 million miles from the Sun. Only Mercury and Venus are closer to the Sun.

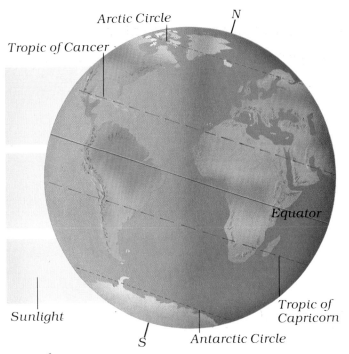

The Sun's rays have to travel farther to reach the Poles than to get to the equator. The rays lose more heat, so the Poles are colder.

What is the Earth's axis?

Take an orange and push a stick through its middle. The stick marks the axis of the orange. There is, of course, no stick through the Earth—its axis is an imaginary line between the Poles. The Earth's axis is tilted about 23.5° from the vertical.

Why do we have day and night?

The Earth rotates, or spins, on its axis as it orbits the Sun; therefore part of the Earth is in sunlight (day) while part is in shadow (night). Since the Earth rotates all the time, day and night follow each other continually. Sunrise marks the start of day and sunset the coming of night.

Is the Earth a unique planet?

No other planet orbiting the Sun is like the Earth. Only the Earth has the necessary conditions for life (as we know it) to exist.

What is the great circle?

This is an imaginary line, like the equator, on the Earth's surface dividing the planet in half.

One day

Earth turns once on its axis.

One lunar month

Moon travels once around Earth

One year

Earth travels once around Sun

A day is the time it takes for the Earth to spin once on its axis. A lunar month (28 days) is the time it takes for the Moon to orbit the Earth, and a year is the time it takes for the Earth to travel around the Sun.

Are our days getting longer?

The Earth spins once on its axis in 23 hours, 56 minutes, and 4.09 seconds. Scientists call this a sidereal day. But the Earth's spin is slowing down, so our days are getting longer. About 400 million years ago, a day on Earth lasted only 22 hours.

How far is the Earth's orbit around the Sun?

The Earth travels 595 million miles around the Sun in 365 days, 6 hours, and 9 minutes. This is called a sidereal year.

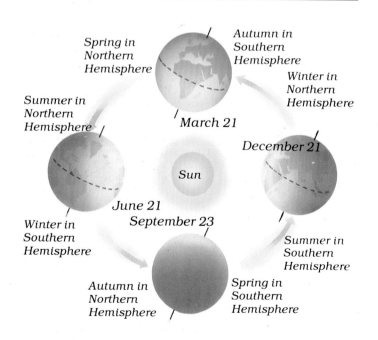

Spring in Northern Hemisphere

Autumn in Southern Hemisphere

Winter in Northern Hemisphere

Summer in Northern Hemisphere

March 21

December 21

Sun

June 21

September 23

Winter in Southern Hemisphere

Summer in Southern Hemisphere

Autumn in Northern Hemisphere

Spring in Southern Hemisphere

Does anybody have the right time?

There is no such thing as Earth-time, because when one place has day, another place on the planet is having night. The world has 24 time zones, and the clock time in each zone differs by one hour from the time in the next. Noon in Greenwich, England, is 7 A.M. in New York (five hours earlier) and 3 P.M. (three hours later) in Moscow. Travelers crossing time zones must reset their watches to local time when they reach their destination.

Which parts of the Earth have the longest summer and winter days?

The length of time that part of the Earth has daylight varies depending on where it is. This is because the Earth's axis is tilted at an angle to its path around the Sun. In midsummer in the Arctic (facing the Sun), it is always daylight, and northern Europe and North America have long summer days. In the Antarctic, it is always night. In midwinter it is the other way around; the Antarctic has permanent daylight, while the Arctic is in darkness, and northern Europe and North America have short winter days.

Why do we have seasons?

The seasons (spring, summer, autumn, winter) occur because the Earth shows different faces to the Sun at different times during its orbit. As the Earth moves around the Sun, the part of it tilted toward the Sun is warmer and has summer; meanwhile the part tilted away from the Sun has winter.

The equinoxes (when the Sun crosses the equator) mark the start of spring and autumn. The Sun is north of the equator from the vernal equinox in March until the autumnal equinox in September.

Is the Earth magnetic?

The Earth behaves like a magnet. It has a magnetic field. But there is no giant magnet deep inside the Earth. The core of the Earth is much too hot, and materials such as iron lose their magnetism when they are very hot.

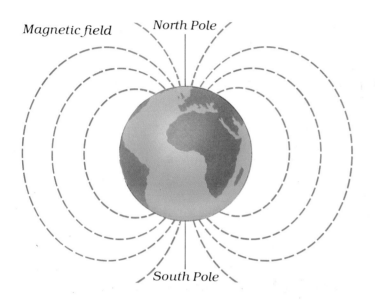

The Earth's magnetic field stretches thousands of miles into space. Like all magnets the field has north and south poles.

How is the Earth's magnetic field made?

The Earth acts like a giant dynamo. Movements inside it create electrical currents that make a magnetic field, with north and south poles—like the poles on a bar magnet.

How far does the Earth's magnetic field reach?

The Earth's magnetic field stretches into space for about 36,000 miles. The Sun and the other planets also have magnetic fields.

Where is Magnetic Island?

Off the coast of Queensland, Australia. In 1770 the English explorer Captain James Cook gave the island this name because he thought, wrongly, that deposits of iron on the island were making his ship's compass behave oddly.

Where are the magnetic poles?

Changes in the Earth's magnetic field make the magnetic poles change positions, but they never stray far from the geographical North and South poles. The north magnetic pole is in northern Canada. The south magnetic pole is in Antarctica. About 450 million years ago the south magnetic pole was in the Sahara Desert in Africa.

Can north change into south?

In an ordinary bar magnet, the north and south poles stay the same, but the Earth's magnetic poles reverse. Every 200,000 to 300,000 years, north becomes south and south becomes north. This may be caused by ripples inside the Earth between the core and the mantle (which turns at a faster rate than the core).

Who thought magnetism held the planets in their orbits?

William Gilbert (1540–1603), physician to Elizabeth I, queen of England. He was interested in magnetism and thought that the Earth was a giant magnet (true) and also that magnetic forces held the planets in their orbits around the Sun (not true).

Does a compass needle point to the North Pole?

No. The magnetized needle of a compass always turns to point in the direction of the Earth's north *magnetic* pole. The north magnetic pole is not the same as the geographic North Pole.

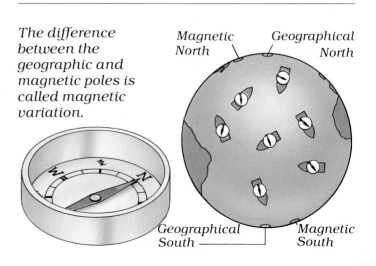

The difference between the geographic and magnetic poles is called magnetic variation.

What is inside the Earth?

The Earth is made of layers of rock. The outer layer is the crust. It is quite thin, between 5 and 25 miles. The next layer down is the mantle, about 1,800 miles thick. The outer core, below the mantle, is about 1,400 miles thick. The inner core is about 800 miles deep.

Is the Earth solid?

The crust is solid, but the rocks of the mantle are so hot that they are partly molten, rather like hot tar. The outer core is hotter still (between 8,000°F and 11,000°F) and is completely molten and liquid. At the very center is a ball of hot rock, squashed so tightly that it is solid.

Could we dig right through to the other side of the Earth?

The Earth's core is much too hot and much too solid to drill through, even if it were possible to drill that far—about 3,200 miles beneath our feet. The deepest drilled hole is one made on the Kola Peninsula by Russian scientists. Drilling began in 1970, but the hole has only reached 7 miles deep so far. The target is 9 miles.

How much of the Earth is water?

The Earth's surface is about 71 percent water. Water on the Earth includes oceans, ice, and water vapor in the atmosphere. This water makes up the Earth's *hydrosphere.*

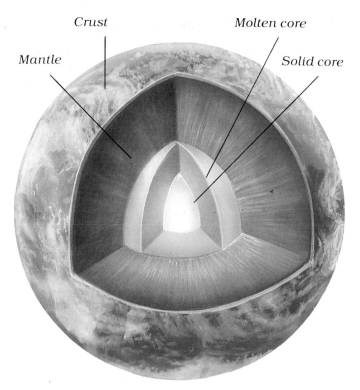

Inside the Earth: the thin crust rests on the mainly solid mantle. Underneath is the molten outer core and the solid inner core.

What is the biosphere?

The biosphere is the Earth's "coat" of air, water, and soil. This is the life layer of the planet. Within the biosphere live all the plants, animals, and other organisms on Earth. No other planet in the Solar System has a similar life-giving biosphere.

Where is the Earth's crust thickest?

The Earth's crust is at its thickest under the continents, or land masses—it averages between 18 and 24 miles thick. Under the oceans, the crust is much thinner—between 3.5 and 5 miles thick.

A cross section through the oceans shows many features of the sea floor, including deep ocean trenches, flat-topped mountains called guyots, and islands formed by underwater volcanoes.

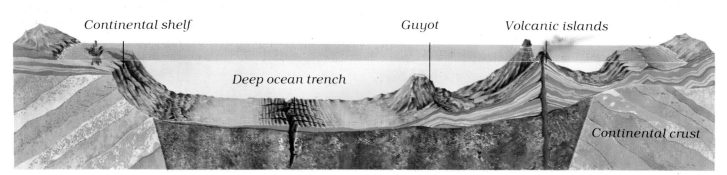

Where were the oldest rocks found?

In 1984 ancient rocks were found in the Northwest Territories of Canada. Scientists believe they are 3.9 billion years old. Even older rocks were discovered in the desert in Chile in 1991. They are iron fragments from a meteorite that hit the Earth about 3.5 billion years ago. The meteorite probably broke off from an asteroid formed at about the same time as the Earth. That makes its rock fragments about 4.3 billion years old—the oldest rocks found on Earth.

How many shooting stars can you see?

On a clear night you will almost certainly see a shooting star or meteor. It looks like a streak of light in the night sky. A shooting star is caused by a pebble-sized rocky particle called a meteoroid hurtling into the Earth's atmosphere from space. As it hits the atmosphere, it burns up. Sometimes as many as a hundred meteors shoot across the sky in an hour.

A meteorite is a lump of stone or metal from outer space. It has survived being burned up as it shoots through the atmosphere to land on Earth.

Where is the biggest meteorite on Earth?

Meteorites are large enough to survive crashing through the atmosphere, but they are not often very big. The biggest one known was found in Namibia, southwest Africa, in 1920. It is over 7 feet across and weighs 66 tons. Larger meteorites have hit the Earth, but they exploded into fragments.

What are meteorites made of?

There are two main types of meteorites. Stony ones are made of rock and may be bits of asteroids that shattered in collisions. Iron meteorites are made of iron or iron-nickel alloy. One rare kind of meteorite contains carbon. Meteorites have remained unchanged since the formation of the Solar System.

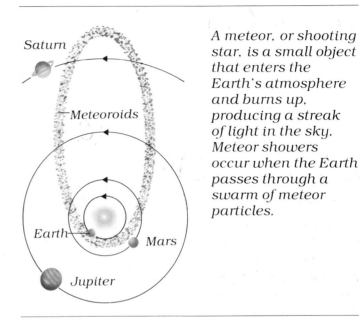

A meteor, or shooting star, is a small object that enters the Earth's atmosphere and burns up, producing a streak of light in the sky. Meteor showers occur when the Earth passes through a swarm of meteor particles.

What can meteorites do to the Earth?

There are craters (ring-shaped holes) in different parts of the world caused by objects from space hitting the Earth. In Arizona there is a crater almost a mile across, made by an object weighing more than 2 million tons. A much larger crater 145 miles wide in Antarctica must have been made by a meteorite weighing more than 14 billion tons.

What was the strange explosion of 1908?

On June 30, 1908, there was a colossal explosion in Siberia. The shock waves were felt 600 miles away. Whole forests were flattened. Was it a giant meteorite? Or an alien starship crashing to Earth? Most scientists believe the explosion was caused by a huge meteorite.

Are the oldest rocks as old as the Earth?

Earth is about 4.6 billion years old, but no Earth rocks of this age have ever been found. The oldest rocks ever discovered are about 4.3 billion years old.

Geography

What do geographers do?

Geographers study the Earth, its features, and living things. They look at the Earth's landscapes—where people, animals, and plants live. They study such features as rivers and deserts. They study where cities are built, what industries produce, and how humans and nature alter the landscape. Some become specialists, such as plant geographers, or oceanographers who study the ocean floor.

How do geographers work?

Geographers travel around the Earth, studying the landscape, making maps, and asking people questions about how they live. They use technology such as radar and aerial photography from aircraft and space satellites. Using survey equipment, they make precise measurements of the Earth's features. From these measurements, accurate maps of various kinds are made. Geographers help plan the cities and countrysides in which we live.

Who were the first geographers?

The ancient Greeks were the first people to study geography as a science, over 2,500 years ago. Our word geography comes from the Greek word *geographia*, which means "description of the Earth."

Who was the most famous geographer of ancient times?

Ptolemy of Alexandria, a Greek scientist, was the most famous geographer of ancient times. The maps of the world that he made around A.D. 150 were studied for centuries after his death, even though they were not very accurate.

When was the Earth first measured?

About 200 B.C. the Greek scientist Eratosthenes measured the distance around the Earth. He studied the angle of the Sun's rays at different places that were a known distance apart. Using geometry, he worked out the Earth's circumference as 252,000 stadia (about 27,600 miles). The modern figure for the Earth's greatest circumference is 24,902 miles.

When were the first maps made?

People probably drew rough maps of their own lands over 5,000 years ago. A clay tablet made in about 2,500 B.C. in Babylonia (now part of Iraq) appears to show what looks like a river valley with mountains on either side. The Egyptians also made maps. Each year the Nile River flooded and washed away boundary markers, so new maps were made to stop arguments over land ownership.

Who invented latitude and longitude?

A map has a network of lines across it. The lines running east-west are lines of latitude, or parallels. The north-south lines are lines of longitude, or meridians. It is easier to find a place on the map by using the lines. Ptolemy was the first map-maker to draw such lines.

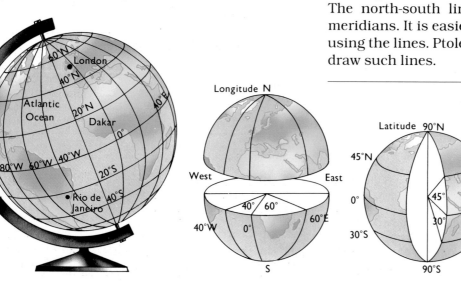

Lines of longitude run north-south on a globe or map. Lines of latitude run east-west. They are measured in degrees.

Old maps of the world often show pictures of sea monsters and strange animals. Most early European maps were based on travelers' tales.

What do degrees measure?

A degree is a small unit of measurement. On maps, 1 degree (1°) is 1/360th of a circle. The lines of longitude and latitude circle the globe, and they are measured in degrees.

What do map scales tell us?

A map is a small picture of a large area. To be accurate, it must be drawn to scale: for example, 1 inch on a world map might represent 1 million inches, or nearly 16 miles, on the ground. This is a scale of 1:1,000,000. A more detailed map, showing perhaps the whole of Spain, might have a scale of 1:100,000. In this case 1 inch on the map represents 100,000 inches, or about half a mile, on the ground.

When did America first appear on maps?

Before 1500, maps made in Europe did not show America. It was unknown to Europeans until Columbus and other European explorers sailed across the Atlantic Ocean in 1492. Soon, however, map-makers began to show the coast and islands of the eastern Americas. The name America was first used on a German map in 1507.

How did Ptolemy's maps mislead Columbus?

Ptolemy's maps showed Europe and China divided by only a narrow sea. In 1492 Columbus set sail westward to cross that sea. Instead of reaching China, he discovered that beyond the wide Atlantic Ocean lay a new continent, America.

When did sailors first use maps?

The first charts (sea maps) were made in Europe in the 1300s. They were called portolan charts and showed the Mediterranean coast in some detail. Sailors could recognize bays and headlands. A web of lines joined the various ports shown on the map, to help sailors find the correct course or direction.

How is height shown on a map?

Altitude, or height, is difficult to show on a flat map. Color shading shows areas that are the same altitude above sea level in the same colors. Contour lines on a map also show altitude. The closer together contour lines are, the steeper the slope on the ground.

Colors on a relief map indicate altitude.

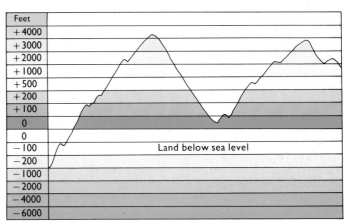

This map was made in Italy in about 1489.

What were early maps like?

Before about 1400 most maps were sketchy. The people who drew them often had only travelers' tales to guide them. They left large areas blank, because little was known about them. Much of Africa, for example, was empty on maps before the 1800s. Map-makers drew pictures of the unknown peoples and imaginary wild beasts that were supposed to live in these lands.

What is a map projection?

No flat map can be entirely accurate because the Earth's surface is curved. A map projection is a means of representing the curved surface on a flat map.

What is cartography?

Cartography is another name for map-making. The word cartography comes from the French word *carte*, which means map. A person who makes maps is a cartographer.

What is Mercator projection?

This is a type of map projection that can be imagined by wrapping a cylindrical roll of paper around a globe. It was made popular (though not invented) by the Flemish map-maker Gerardus Mercator (1512–1594). It is often used for world maps.

How did a Mercator map aid sailors?

Maps using Mercator projection show the exact direction from one place to another. This is because their lines of latitude run at right angles to the lines of longitude. Such maps made it possible for sailors to chart a more accurate course.

Which is the only really accurate way of mapping the Earth?

On a globe, which is the same shape as the Earth itself. You can see this for yourself by drawing a simple Earth map on an orange with a pen. Peel the orange, and then spread out the peel. As you flatten it, your map is stretched out of shape: it becomes distorted. On a flat map some features of the Earth are shown accurately, but others may be the wrong size in relation to other features.

Cylindrical map projections fit a cylinder of paper around a globe. The lines of latitude and longitude on the map are straight. This type of projection is known as Mercator projection.

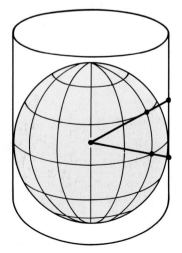

Mercator projection

How are modern maps made?

Most maps are made from photographs taken from aircraft or from satellites orbiting the Earth. They show the land and sea in great detail. Until the 1970s only a quarter of Peru had been properly mapped. A satellite took enough pictures in three minutes to complete the work!

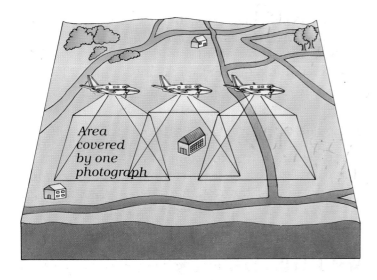

Aerial photographs are used to make accurate maps. Each photograph slightly overlaps the next, so no detail is lost.

Why does Greenland look too big on some maps?

On a map using Mercator projection, the lines of longitude are straightened out so that they are parallel instead of meeting at the Poles. This makes the Poles look too far apart. It also "stretches" parts of the world, making Greenland look as big as North America, when it is actually smaller.

Who gives places their names on maps?

All peoples use their own names for places. An example is Vienna (English), which is Wien in German, Vienne in French, and Becs in Hungarian. Explorers often asked local people the name of a place, but misunderstood the reply. (Some curious place names on maps translate into English as "I don't know!") The British Royal Geographical Society and the United States Board on Geographic Names are among organizations that try to standardize the names used on maps.

When did people think the world was flat?

In the past, many people thought the Earth was flat and that ships could fall off the edge of the world if they sailed too far. The ancient Greeks and Chinese thought the Earth was round. People watching a distant ship's mast appear on the ocean horizon before the rest of the vessel came into view may also have suspected that the world was round.

How did atlases get their name?

An atlas is a collection of maps in a book. The name was first used in the 1500s, when many map books had a picture of the legendary giant Atlas at the front. According to Greek legends, Atlas was defeated by Zeus, King of the Gods, and forced to hold the heavens on his shoulders.

What is the difference between a physical map and a political map?

A physical map show features such as rivers and mountains. A political map shows the geographical boundaries of the various countries and their major towns.

A political map shows the geographical boundaries of each country.

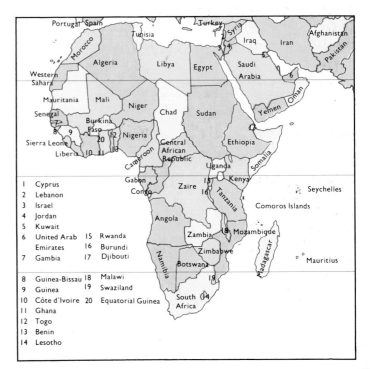

Structure

What are the elements?

Everything on the Earth is made of elements. An element is a substance made of only one kind of atom. It is impossible to break up an element into parts that have different chemical properties.

Which is the Earth's most common element?

Oxygen is the most common element in the Earth's crust by weight (about 50 percent). Next is silicon, about 28 percent by weight.

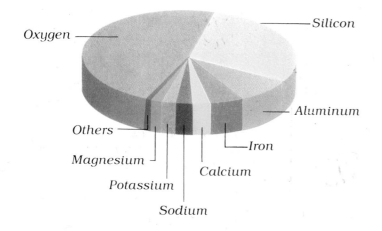

Oxygen makes up the biggest slice of the Earth's crust, followed by silicon, aluminum, and iron. The other main ingredients of the crust are shown on the pie chart.

What was the "universal element"?

About 600 B.C. a Greek scientist named Thales thought that all matter—that which the Earth is made of—was made of water. Water was considered the universal element.

Who thought the Earth was made of just four elements?

Aristotle (384–322 B.C.) decided that everything was made of four elements: fire, air, earth, and water. People went on believing this was true for over a thousand years.

How many elements are there?

There are 92 elements found in nature. Some elements, such as copper, gold, and iron, have been known and used for thousands of years. Most elements were only isolated (discovered in their pure form) after the 1700s. Besides the 92 natural elements, there are others that can be made only in laboratories during atomic reactions. So far 109 elements have been isolated.

What are the three states of matter?

The three states in which matter exists are solid, liquid, and gas. Water, for example, is liquid at normal temperatures. It changes to a gas (water vapor, or steam) when heated. When it is cooled below the freezing point (32°F), it becomes a solid (ice).

Water can exist as a solid (ice), a liquid (water), or a gas (water vapor). In each state the molecules behave differently. As the temperature rises, the molecules move faster and farther apart.

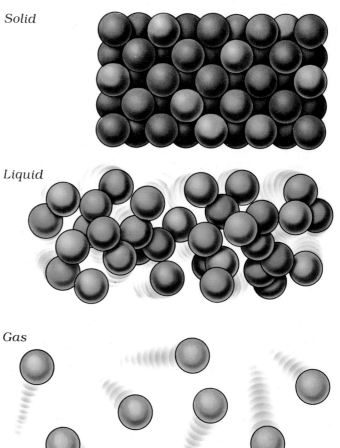

Solid

Liquid

Gas

What are minerals?

The Earth's rocks are made up of materials called minerals. Some, such as gold, are made of only one element. Others, such as salt, are made of two or more elements. Some minerals are metals—copper, for example. Sulfur, diamond, and graphite are minerals that are not metals.

What is a compound?

A compound is a substance made of two or more elements combined in such a way that you cannot separate them easily. Water is an example of a compound. It is made of hydrogen and oxygen. The hydrogen and oxygen atoms are joined by invisible forces called bonds.

Which element forms the most compounds?

About 95 percent of all compounds contain the element carbon. Carbon is the only element with atoms that join together readily to form chains, rings, and other structures. There are almost 4 million carbon compounds. Most of these compounds also contain the element hydrogen.

Copper is mined in many countries. The Bingham Canyon open-pit copper mine in Utah is the largest open-pit mine in the United States.

What are diamonds made of?

Diamond is a form of carbon. It is the hardest substance known. Carbon is found in other substances, such as coal, petroleum, and limestone. Carbon exists in the atmosphere as a gas (carbon dioxide).

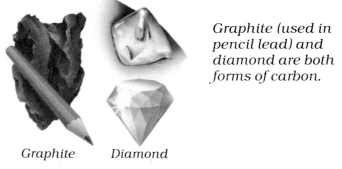

Graphite (used in pencil lead) and diamond are both forms of carbon.

Graphite   Diamond

How many compounds are there?

There are more than 6.8 million compounds. Only about 65,000 have common uses.

How are crystals formed?

Crystals are solids that are found in nature in many shapes and sizes. Most minerals and metals are crystalline. Look at sugar through a magnifying glass. You will see that the sugar is made up of thousands of tiny, glassy pieces. These are sugar crystals.

There are seven main types of crystals, based on the number, shape, and angle of the crystal faces.

Calcite
(hexagonal)

Pyrite
(cubic)

Gypsum
(monoclinic)

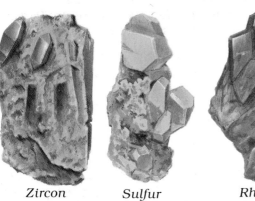

Zircon
(tetragonal)

Sulfur
(orthorhombic)

Rhodonite
(triclinic)

How can you make crystals?

You can "grow" crystals for yourself using a mineral such as salt. Sprinkle the salt slowly into a bowl of hot water, stirring all the time to dissolve it. After a while, no more salt will dissolve. Cool the water (which is now a solution, *saturated* with the salt). Rest a stick across the bowl and hang a thread or string from it, with the end dangling in the solution. Crystals will begin to form on the thread or string.

How are all snowflakes alike?

Snowflakes are crystals of frozen water. Under a microscope, you can see that snowflakes reveal many astonishing shapes. Yet each flake has the same number of sides or branches: six. Snowflakes are six-sided crystals.

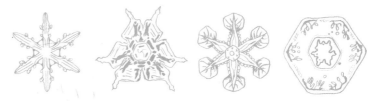

Snowflakes are crystals. They form in many beautiful patterns, yet each crystal has just six sides or branches.

What is a metal?

There are two basic groups of elements: metals and nonmetals. More than 70 of the elements are metals. The most commonly used are iron, copper, and aluminum.

Which is the most common metal?

The metal found most abundantly in the Earth's crust is aluminum. It makes up about 8 percent of the crust. Aluminum is not found pure but in the form of bauxite. Bauxite is an ore—a substance containing not only metal but also other materials such as oxygen, sulfur, and carbon.

How can you tell a metal is a metal?

Most metals are shiny. All metals except mercury are solid at room temperature. Most are malleable (they can be pressed or hammered into thin sheets) and ductile (they can be drawn out into wire and bent without cracking). Most of the metals used in industry are alloys, or mixtures, such as bronze and steel. These alloys are stronger than the pure metals from which they are made.

What is metallurgy?

Metallurgy is the branch of chemistry that studies metals. Metallurgists study how metals are separated from their ores and also the structure and properties of metals.

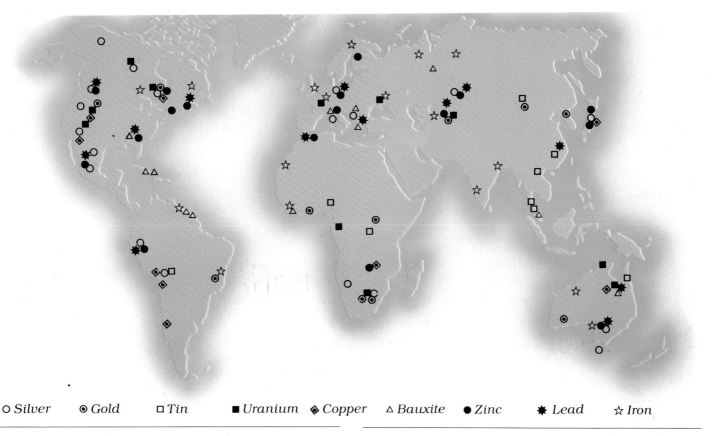

○ *Silver*   ◉ *Gold*   □ *Tin*   ■ *Uranium*   ◈ *Copper*   △ *Bauxite*   ● *Zinc*   ✸ *Lead*   ☆ *Iron*

Which is the heaviest metal?

The heaviest metal is osmium, which is 22 times as heavy as water. Osmium is twice as heavy as lead. The lightest metal is lithium, which is only half as heavy as water.

Where do metals come from?

Metals are found in the ground, though seldom in their pure form. Many metals occur in combination with other elements in minerals. These minerals are known as ores. The ore must be treated, for example by heating, to get rid of the other elements and extract the pure metal.

Who believed moistness made metals?

This idea was put forward by Aristotle in ancient Greece and was believed into the Middle Ages. Aristotle thought that under the ground there were dry "exhalations," which made soils and stones, and moist ones, which made metals.

Droplets of mercury look shiny because their curved surfaces reflect light, like mirrors.

This map shows known metal deposits throughout the world. However, there are likely many more still to be discovered.

What is mercury?

Mercury (also known as quicksilver) is an unusual metal which is liquid at normal temperatures. It is very poisonous. Drops of mercury look like small, shiny beads. Mercury can be poured out of a flask, like water, but unlike water, it leaves no droplets or film behind; the sides of the flask are left perfectly clean and dry.

EVER-CHANGING EARTH

How many continents are there?

A continent is a landmass surrounded or almost surrounded by water. There are seven continents: Africa, Antarctica, Asia, Australia, Europe, North America, and South America.

Who first wondered if the continents fitted together?

Accurate maps of both the Old and New Worlds were not made until the 1500s. Sir Francis Bacon noticed that the coasts of eastern America and western Africa might fit together like pieces of a puzzle.

Which is the biggest continent?

The biggest continent is Asia, which has a total land area of 17 million square miles—four times bigger than Europe and almost twice the size of North America.

What was the supercontinent?

About 200 million years ago, there was one vast landmass on the Earth. This supercontinent is known as Pangaea. Around it was an enormous ocean, which has been named the Tethys Sea.

The Earth's continents

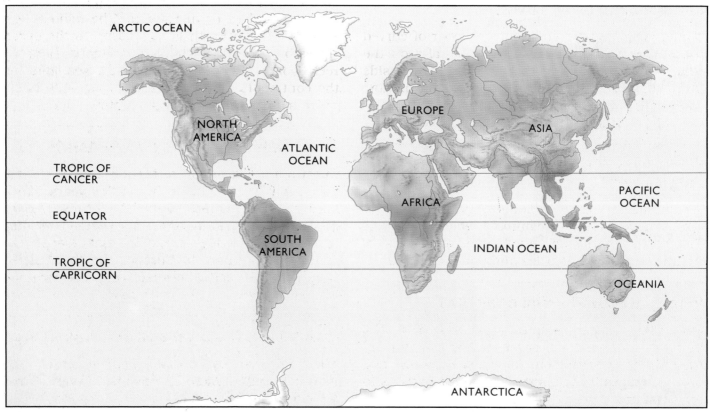

20

Where did the supercontinent go?

The ancient supercontinent, Pangaea, split into two continents—Laurasia and Gondwanaland—about 200 million years ago. About 65 million years ago, Laurasia and Gondwanaland broke up into smaller pieces. These pieces drifted apart and began to look like the continents we know today. This process is called *continental drift.*

200 million years ago

100 million years ago

50 million years ago

About 200 million years ago the single continent split into smaller land masses, and, after millions of years, the continents we know today were formed.

Present day

Can the continents move?

The Earth's crust is made of a number of curved rocky plates. These plates float like rafts on the molten mantle underneath. Heat from deep inside the Earth makes currents move through the mantle. These currents make the plates move, and they carry the continents that rest on top of them.

When were Antarctica and Texas neighbors?

Mountains in Antarctica and the southwest United States have much in common. Scientists think that North America was once joined to Antarctica, wedged between Antarctica and South America.

What is the continental crust like?

The Earth's crust is thin for its size. Imagine the Earth as a football; the crust would be no thicker than a postage stamp stuck on it. The continental crust averages 25 miles thick. The lower rocks in the crust are red-hot.

What makes the sea floor spread?

Another clue to why the continents move is found on the sea floor. Here there are deep trenches and midocean ridges or mountains. The molten rock deep inside the Earth is carried up to the ocean ridges by currents in the syrupy mantle. Here the rock cools and hardens, pushing the sea floor and the continents away from the ridges. This movement is known as sea-floor spreading.

When will Australia bump into Asia?

Experts on continental drift think that the Earth will look very different in 50 million years. North America and South America will have broken apart. Australia will drift northward, possibly colliding with Asia. The Mediterranean Sea may disappear as Africa moves closer to Europe, and the Atlantic Ocean will get bigger because South America and Africa will have drifted farther apart.

How thick is the crust beneath mountains?

The crust reaches its thickest point under high mountain ranges. Here the crust is between 36 and 42 miles thick.

Rocks

What is geology?

Geology is the study of the Earth's history. Geologists study features such as rocks, caves, and mountains. They want to know how the Earth was made and how it changes.

Geologists study the Earth's rocks.

How is the Earth always changing?

Since the Earth was formed over 4.5 billion years ago, it has changed in many ways. Some changes happen so slowly that they are not noticeable in a person's lifetime. Earthquakes and volcanoes, however, can alter landscapes in hours. Glaciers, rivers, and oceans can also alter the face of the Earth, but they may take thousands of years.

How do geologists study the structure of the Earth's inside?

We cannot look inside the Earth because light cannot penetrate rock. However, geologists can probe the rocks with shock waves that spread out in all directions. The waves are reflected or refracted (bent, like light rays passing through glass) by the rocks. The shock waves speed up through dense rocks and slow down through less dense rocks, so scientists can measure the rocks' thickness.

What are rocks made of?

Rocks lie beneath the soil, beneath the seas, and beneath the polar ice. Most rocks are aggregates, or combinations of one or more minerals. Under a microscope, you can see the grains of minerals in a slice of rock.

Which is older: land or sea floor?

The rocks of the Earth's continents are about 3.8 billion years old. The oldest rocks in the ocean are younger—less than 200 million years old. At midocean ridges, new rocks are constantly pushed up from inside the Earth.

What are the main kinds of rocks?

There are three main kinds of rocks. Their names describe the ways in which the rocks were formed. They are called igneous, sedimentary, and metamorphic rocks.

What are igneous rocks?

Igneous means "fire-made." Igneous rocks are made from molten rock called magma inside the Earth. Magma is very hot, over 2,000°F, and is under enormous pressure. Sometimes magma is forced to the Earth's surface, where it cools to form igneous rocks.

The three kinds of rocks are formed in different ways.

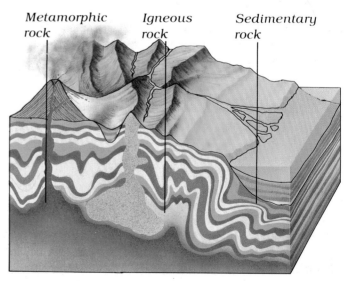

Metamorphic rock   Igneous rock   Sedimentary rock

This picture shows examples of igneous, metamorphic, and sedimentary rocks. Granite, an igneous rock, is one of the hardest. Marble and slate are metamorphic rocks formed from the sedimentary rocks limestone and shale. Obsidian is a natural glass. Pumice is a light, porous rock thrown out when a volcano erupts.

How do volcanoes form rocks?

When a volcano erupts, red-hot streams of magma pour out through cracks and vents in the Earth. In the cooler air, the magma hardens quickly. It forms igneous rocks such as obsidian, which looks like glass, or pumice, which is full of frothy air bubbles. Some volcanic rocks cool more slowly, so that mineral crystals have time to form. You can see such crystals in basalt.

What makes river mud into rocks?

Rocks on the Earth's surface are worn away into tiny grains by water, wind, ice, and other natural forces. Rain washes the grains into rivers, which leave a muddy "sediment" behind wherever they flow most slowly. Sediment piles up in layers that, over millions of years, are pressed down so hard that they become rock. Shale is sedimentary rock made from clay. Sandstone is made from sand.

How do rocks form in blisters?

Magma does not always get pushed right to the surface. It may stop just below the surface, pushing up the rocks above like a blister. It then slowly cools and hardens. Granite is formed in this way.

What turns limestone to marble?

Metamorphosis means "change." Metamorphic rocks have been changed by heat, pressure, or chemical action. Some rocks are heated by magma pushing through them. Others are pressurized by movements of the crust beneath mountains. When limestone is heated and squeezed like this, it changes into marble.

Which tiny animal made Dover's white cliffs?

Chalk is a form of limestone. This is a sedimentary rock made from the skeletons of sea creatures. The white cliffs of Dover in England are made of limestone chalk formed from the shells of tiny one-celled animals called foraminifera.

Foraminifera

Caves and tunnels are formed in limestone rock through the action of rainwater. Streams enter from the surface (1) and emerge near the base (5). Stalactites (2), stalagmites (3), and columns (4) form as dissolved limestone is deposited by dripping water.

Which is the most common kind of rock?

Sedimentary rocks form about 75 percent of the Earth's land surface, even though they make up only a small part of the total crust.

Can rain leave marks on rock?

Sedimentary rocks were once soft mud or sand. Some rocks still have ripple marks, showing that they were once under the sea. Other rocks have marks made by raindrops hitting the soft mud or sand before it hardened.

Can rocks be folded?

Sedimentary rocks are laid down in layers called strata or beds. The layers look like a giant "multi-decker" sandwich. When the Earth's crust moves, the "sandwich" may be bent and squashed. The layers of rock are broken and folded, bringing rocks from deep down up to the Earth's surface.

What are batholiths?

Masses of igneous rock formed deep in the Earth are called batholiths. Parts of such rock formations may be exposed at the Earth's surface.

How are caves made?

Most caves are hollowed out of rock by underground water. The water trickles down from the Earth's surface, dissolving some of the rock to form small passages and openings. Carbon dioxide in the air can make the water slightly acidic, and this acid eats away at the rock. Streams may also flow into and through the cave, making it bigger.

What is a sinkhole?

Some caves have a vertical entrance leading straight down into them. This is a sinkhole and is caused by the cave roof collapsing. Other caves have mouths on hillsides or valley slopes. A stream often flows out through this opening.

Where are the world's longest caves?

The longest cave system explored is the Mammoth-Flint Ridge cave system in Kentucky. There are more than 190 miles of caves, many linked by passages. It was first explored in 1799.

Are all caves small and narrow?

People who explore caves (known as cavers, pot-holers, or spelunkers) often have to scramble on hands and knees inside narrow cave passages. Some caves, however, are as big as several football fields! In Sarawak, Malaysia, there is a cave chamber 2,300 feet long, 1,000 feet wide, and 230 feet high. Some of the biggest and most spectacular caves are tourist attractions.

What was found inside the Lascaux Cave?

This cave is in southwest France. It contains remarkably well preserved wall paintings made many thousands of years ago by Stone Age artists. In prehistoric times people often made their homes in caves, for shelter and protection from wild animals. Some caves were used by generations after generations of people.

How can we tell stalactites from stalagmites?

Stalactites and stalagmites form inside limestone caves. The water that drips steadily from the roof contains a mineral called calcite. The water dries, but the calcite remains and slowly builds into a column. Stalactites grow downward, from the cave roof. Stalagmites grow upward, from the cave floor. Sometimes the two columns meet to form a pillar.

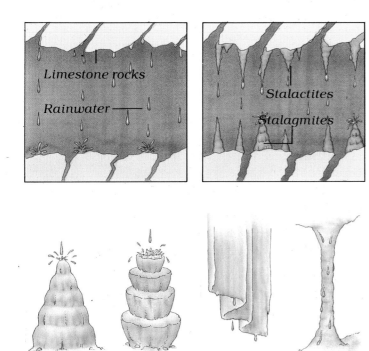

Limestone rocks

Rainwater

Stalactites

Stalagmites

Fir cone stalagmite   Dish stack stalagmite   Drape stalactite   Column

How stalactites and stalagmites grow inside caves. They can form various strange shapes.

Who might enter a pothole?

Cavers enter potholes. A pothole is an opening in the ground, usually in limestone rock, worn away by water.

Why is the Blue Grotto blue?

The Blue Grotto is a famous sea cave on the Mediterranean island of Capri, Italy. The cave gets its name from the effect of the sunlight shining through its waters; the entire cave is filled with sapphire blue light.

What are stone flowers?

Some dissolved minerals can form flowerlike shapes in caves. Gypsum flowers are crystals that look like delicate flowers growing out of the rock. Other growths look like twisted mushrooms.

Where are the Carlsbad Caverns?

These caves are in New Mexico and contain some of the biggest stalactites and stalagmites in the world.

What do geologists mean by "faults"?

A fault is a crack cutting through layers of rocks. Pressure on the crack causes movement, which is felt as an earthquake. Rocks on each side of the fault may shift up or down or slide past each other.

How did coal form?

The coal we burn as fuel is found in seams, or layers, under the ground. It was formed millions of years ago from the remains of dead plants. The plants formed layers of peat, which in time were buried beneath sand and mud. The sand and mud formed rocks, and the weight of the rocks pressing down on the peat layers changed the peat into coal.

Coal was formed from prehistoric plants. The plants were covered with layers of sand and mud that eventually crushed them into coal.

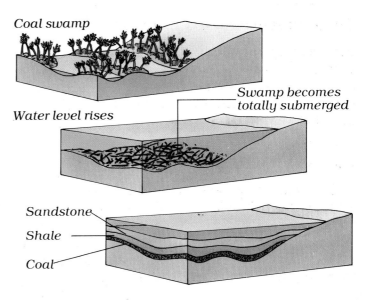

Coal swamp

Water level rises

Swamp becomes totally submerged

Sandstone

Shale

Coal

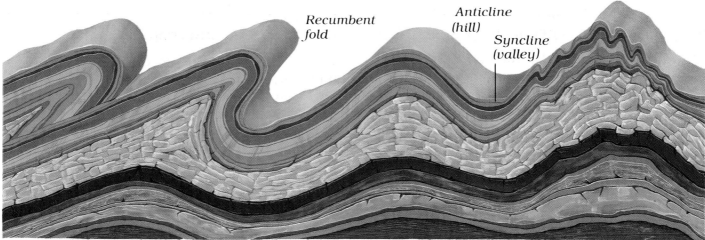

Recumbent fold

Anticline (hill)

Syncline (valley)

Simple folding produces hills and valleys.

How are mountains made?

There are three main types of mountains, each made in different ways. They are volcanoes, fold mountains, and fault-block mountains.

How high is Mount Everest?

The highest mountain above sea level is Mount Everest in the Himalayas. Working out the exact height of such great mountains in remote regions is difficult. In 1860 surveyors calculated that Everest was 29,002 feet high. In 1973 this was corrected to 29,028 feet. In 1987 satellite measurements gave the height of Mount Everest as 29,293 feet.

Mount Everest in the Himalaya range of Asia is the highest point on Earth.

How high is the Earth's tallest mountain?

The highest mountain on Earth is the island peak of Mauna Kea in Hawaii. This great mountain rises 33,476 feet from the Pacific Ocean floor, but only 13,796 feet of it is above water.

When did the Alps appear?

The European Alps are fold mountains, formed when land masses to the north and south moved closer together. The rock layers were squashed up into folds, making mountains. A vast sea once covered the land where the Alps now are. The mountains were formed about 15 million years ago.

Which are older: high or low mountains?

High mountain ranges are younger than old ranges. Old ranges have been slowly worn away by wind, rain, and other natural forces of erosion and are therefore fairly low. High mountain ranges were formed more recently, and for them the wearing-down process has only just begun.

What kind of mountains make the Sierra Nevada?

The Sierra Nevada mountains in North America are fault-block mountains. Fault-block mountains form along faults, which are breaks in the Earth's crust. When there is an earthquake, huge blocks of rock are pushed up or tilted beneath the faults. Mountains are raised up in this way.

Where are the world's highest mountains?

The highest mountains of the world are found in long ranges such as the Himalayas (Asia), the Andes (South America), and the Rockies (North America).

Which mountain range has the highest peaks?

The world's 20 highest mountains are all in the Himalaya-Karakoram range in Asia. They are all over 26,000 feet high.

Why are high mountaintops covered in snow?

High mountaintops are surrounded by very cold air. For every 1,000 feet in height, the temperature falls by about 12°F. The highest mountains are snow-covered all year round. Even in midsummer the air is always freezing cold.

How high are the Andes?

The Andes have the highest mountains in the Western Hemisphere. There are more than 50 peaks above 20,000 feet. The highest is Cerro Aconcagua in Argentina, an extinct (dead) volcano 22,831 feet high.

What is a mountain range?

A group of mountains is called a range. Most mountains are found in ranges, although some are single peaks, such as lone volcanoes. Several ranges form a mountain system. The Pacific Mountain System in North America includes several ranges such as the Sierra Nevada, the Cascade Range, and the Alaska Range.

Does Everest have any close rivals?

Some people have argued that K2, another Himalayan mountain, is higher than Everest. However, according to the most recent measurements by satellite, K2, also known as Godwin Austen or Chogori, is only 28,250 feet high.

Which is the world's steepest mountain?

Many high mountains have sheer rock walls in places but are more gently sloping elsewhere. The steepest mountain is probably Mount Rakaposhi in Pakistan. It soars to a height of 20,000 feet in a distance of 32,810 feet—a gradient of 1 in 1.6 (1 foot up for every 1.6 feet forward). It is 25,500 feet high from base to peak.

The Earth's highest mountain peaks

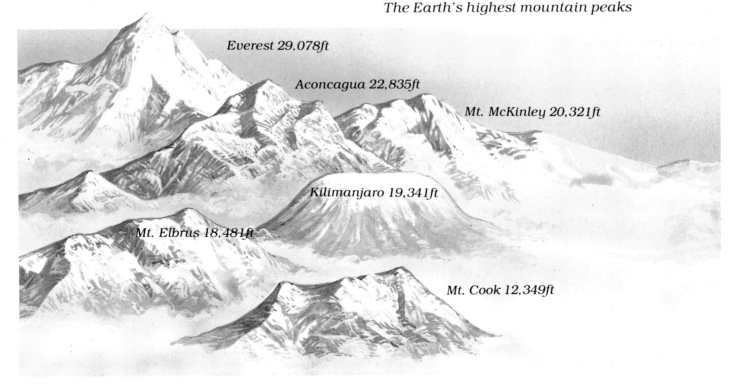

Everest 29,078ft

Aconcagua 22,835ft

Mt. McKinley 20,321ft

Kilimanjaro 19,341ft

Mt. Elbrus 18,481ft

Mt. Cook 12,349ft

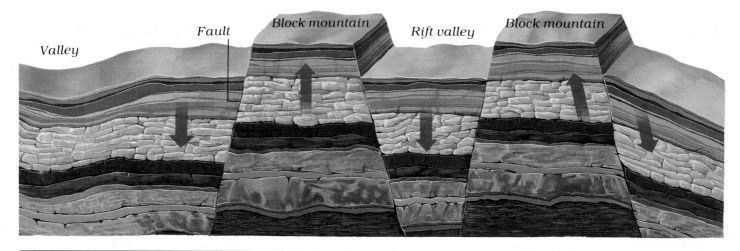

Valley   *Fault*   *Block mountain*   *Rift valley*   *Block mountain*

What makes a landslide?

Landslides are falls of rock and mud sent cascading down a mountain or hillside. The cause is often an earthquake or volcanic eruption. The violent movement of the Earth causes loose or wet surface material to break away and slide downhill. A big landslide can bury a valley and destroy towns.

An avalanche crashes down a mountain slope.

A block mountain is pushed up between faults. A rift valley sinks between faults.

What is a rift valley?

A rift valley is a long valley formed when a block of land collapses between two faults. The best example is the Great Rift Valley, which runs from north to south along much of eastern Africa. Movement along the faults means that millions of years from now a large chunk of East Africa will split away from the rest of the continent.

What is an avalanche?

Sometimes a huge mass of snow slides down a mountain side. This is an avalanche. Avalanches happen when the snow on the mountain is disturbed by wind, earth movements, loud noises, or even by people skiing. The avalanche gets bigger as it slides down the mountain, carrying with it rocks and fallen trees. Dry snow avalanches move faster than wet snow—at over 100 miles per hour.

What is a volcano?

A volcano is a vent or hole in the Earth's crust. Through the vent, hot molten rocks from deep inside the Earth pour out onto the surface. The volcano acts like a safety valve, releasing some of the enormous forces that build up inside the Earth.

What is an active volcano?

An active volcano erupts often. A volcano that may erupt, but does so infrequently, is called dormant. An extinct volcano will not erupt again.

What happens when a volcano erupts?

When a volcano erupts, magma (molten rock) from deep inside the Earth is pushed up toward the surface. Red-hot lava (the name given to magma when it pours out above ground) flows out of the volcano. Smoke and ash belch upward, darkening the sky.

Why do some volcanoes explode?

An explosive volcano contains very thick lava. The lava is pushed upward very slowly and may form a plug, sealing the volcano. Pressure builds up inside until gas and ash burst through, blowing the top off the volcano in a huge explosion.

How many volcanoes are there?

There are over 850 known active volcanoes in the world. About 80 of these are under the ocean.

Why do some volcanoes just grumble?

Not all volcanoes explode violently. Some just grumble. The lava inside them wells up slowly, so there is time for the hot gases to trickle out instead of bursting out. The fluid lava can flow out around the volcano to form a large sloping dome.

What is a volcanic bomb?

Thick lava inside a volcano may trap gas bubbles which burst when they are forced to the surface, sending up a shower of "bombs." These rock fragments can be 3 feet across and weigh 100 tons.

Which country has most volcanoes?

Indonesia in Southeast Asia has the greatest number of active volcanoes—about 200. Indonesia is on the so-called "Ring of Fire"—a belt of great volcanic activity around the Pacific Ocean.

An erupting volcano. Molten magma is forced up the volcano's central vent (1). Ash and lava pour out of this and smaller side vents (2). Magma also hardens underground to form dykes (3), sills (4), and laccoliths (5). Geysers (6) are also found in volcanic regions.

The church spire was all that was left of San Juan Parangaricútiro in Mexico after a volcanic eruption in 1943 covered the village with lava.

How quickly can a new volcano grow?

In 1943 a farmer in Mexico noticed a crack in the ground in a cornfield. The crack was the opening of a volcano called Paricutín. The lava oozing from the crack piled up 490 feet high in just six days. For almost ten years the volcano grew, forming a cinder cone over 1,300 feet high.

Do volcanoes do any good?

Volcanoes can cause terrible destruction and loss of life. However, they are also beneficial. Volcanic soil is rich and fertile. That is why people often live on the slopes of volcanoes, despite the danger of eruption. Volcanic rock is also a good material for building roads. The enormous heat generated by volcanoes can be tapped to make electricity or to provide hot water for homes.

Cinder volcanoes (1) throw out ash, building up a low dome. Shield volcanoes (2) are flatter and the lava flows out of several openings.

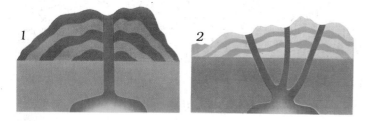

Which is the world's largest active volcano?

The largest volcano that still erupts regularly (it erupted last in 1984) is Mauna Loa in Hawaii. Its dome is 72 miles long and 62 miles across. It has a crater 6 miles wide. Mauna Loa is 13,677 feet high.

When was the greatest known volcanic eruption?

In 1883 the island of Krakatoa, between Java and Sumatra in Indonesia, exploded. This volcanic eruption is thought to have had the power of 26 hydrogen bombs. Dust thrown into the air was carried around the Earth by winds and fell over 3,000 miles away. Huge as the Krakatoa eruption was, scientists believe the volcano that destroyed Santorini, near Crete, in 1628 B.C. was five times more powerful.

What damage did Krakatoa cause?

The explosion of the volcano at Krakatoa caused great loss of life. More than 36,000 people were killed. Most of these were drowned when an ocean wave 130 feet high, caused by the eruption, swept across neighboring islands.

Where is Stromboli?

This is a famous volcano in the Mediterranean Sea, on an island of the same name close to Sicily. It is 3,031 feet high and is one of the few European volcanoes to be constantly active. However, Stromboli is relatively harmless because its lava flows freely all the time. Violent explosions are unlikely because there is no dangerous buildup of pressure inside the volcano. This continuous, nonviolent type of eruption is known as a Strombolian eruption.

Why do volcanoes give off clouds of black smoke?

An erupting volcano belches out huge quantities of gases. These include steam, carbon dioxide, nitrogen, and sulfur dioxide. Carried with the gas are large amounts of volcanic dust. The gas and dust together look like black smoke. The clouds from a big volcanic eruption can blot out the sunlight and affect weather over a wide area.

Why do volcanoes and earthquakes often go together?

Earthquakes and volcanoes often seem to occur together. They happen most often in parts of the Earth where two of the plates making up the crust meet. Rocks are either pushed up to form mountains or ridges or sunk down into the Earth's mantle to create trenches. This movement makes the Earth's surface unstable, and earthquakes and volcanoes are likely to occur.

What causes earthquakes?

Earthquakes happen in places where there are great faults, or cracks, in the rocks below ground. These places are at the edges of the huge plates, or sections, in the Earth's crust. The plates slowly move past or toward each other. Where two plates meet, the rocks on either side of the gap slide past each other, which can make the ground shake.

The power of an earthquake is immense. Some buildings are designed to withstand the shock, but many shake and collapse.

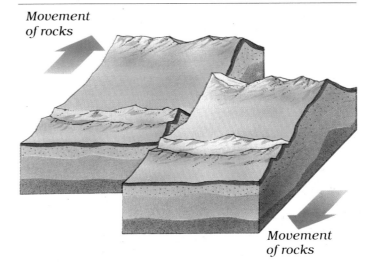

Movement of rocks

Movement of rocks

Earthquakes occur in places where crustal plates move past or toward each other.

What happens in an earthquake?

In an earthquake, the ground begins to shake. The shaking may last for only a few seconds or for minutes. Buildings may shake, crack, and collapse. Surface cracks open up, and whole chunks of land may sink suddenly.

Earthquake zones

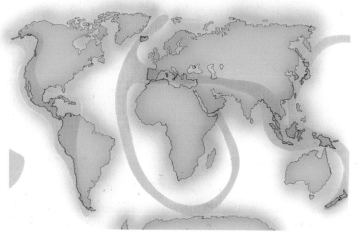

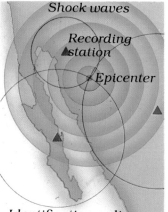

Shock waves

Recording station

Epicenter

Identification radius

Above: The map shows the zones of the Earth where earthquakes occur most frequently.

Left: The most violent shock is felt at an earthquake's epicenter—the point on the Earth's surface above the rock movement.

What was the world's most destructive earthquake?

The earthquake that caused the most destruction hit Japan in 1923. More than 575,000 homes in the cities of Tokyo and Yokohama were destroyed. Fires broke out after the earthquake, causing most of the damage. More than 142,000 people were killed.

Which earthquakes killed the most people?

In 1556 an earthquake at Shaanxi in China killed 800,000 people. An earthquake in 1976 at Tangshan, also in China, killed 750,000 people.

Are earthquakes rare?

No. There are about 500,000 earthquakes every year, but most are too small to be felt. About 1,000 earthquakes a year are powerful enough to cause some damage.

Can scientists tell when earthquakes will happen?

Scientists know the areas of the world where earthquakes are most likely to occur. They can measure small movements along a fault in the rocks. But they cannot yet tell exactly when an earthquake will happen. Scientists who study earthquakes are called seismologists.

How is an earthquake's strength measured?

Scientists use the Richter scale of measurement to compare the strength of earthquakes at their epicenters. The scale ranges from 0 to 12. At 2 on the scale, you would feel a tremor, or shock, beneath your feet. At 6 on the scale, houses are likely to be damaged. An earthquake measuring 8.5 or more is disastrous. Each number on the scale represents an earthquake ten times as strong as the one below it.

Each number on the Richter scale represents an earthquake ten times as strong as the one below: 1. Felt only by seismographs; 2. Feeble; 3. Slight, like heavy trucks passing; 4. Moderate; 5. Quite strong, felt by most people; 6. Strong; 7. Very strong, walls crack; 8. Destructive; 9. Ruinous, houses collapse and pipes crack; 10. Disastrous, ground cracks; 11. Very disastrous; 12. Catastrophic, ground rises and falls in waves.

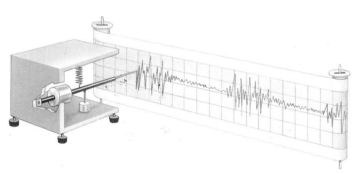

A seismograph

How does a seismograph work?

A seismograph is an instrument for measuring movements under the ground. It can measure the shock waves made by an earthquake. In addition, when scientists set off small explosions to make shock waves underground, a seismograph can help find oil or help measure the thickness of a glacier. A seismograph consists of a frame, inside of which is a weight on a spring. When the earth shakes, the frame moves but the weight does not. A pen fixed to the weight makes a wavy line on a recording chart as the seismograph moves up or down.

Where is the San Andreas Fault?

In California there is a fracture in the Earth's crust over 750 miles long. It is called the San Andreas Fault, and it marks the boundary between two of the Earth's plates: the Pacific Plate and the North American Plate. The plates are sliding past one another, at a speed of about 2 inches a year. In places the plates sometimes lock together and enormous pressure builds up. The result is an earthquake—such as those that hit San Francisco in 1906 and 1989.

What happened to San Francisco in 1906?

The city of San Francisco was badly damaged by an earthquake soon after 5 A.M. on April 18, 1906. Many buildings fell down, but the worst damage was done by fire, started by broken gas pipes and electric cables. The earthquake shattered the city's main water pipes, so fighting the fires was even more difficult. The city then had about 350,000 people. Nearly all of them lost their homes, and about 3,000 people were killed. When the fires were at last put out, more than 28,000 of the city's buildings were in ruins.

What is a geyser?

A geyser is a gushing fountain of hot water. Geysers are found in areas of volcanic activity, such as Iceland. Hot volcanic rocks heat underground water, which bubbles up as a hot spring. If water deeper down is heated further, it turns to steam and pushes up the cooler water above it to form a spout or geyser.

Where is the world's most famous geyser?

In Yellowstone National Park, Wyoming, there is a famous geyser known as Old Faithful. It erupts every 73 minutes, throwing a jet of steaming hot water over 130 feet high. It has never missed a spout in the last 80 years.

Why do geysers sometimes form strange craters?

The water thrown out by a geyser contains dissolved minerals. The water either evaporates or soaks back into the ground, leaving behind deposits of mineral. These deposits can make strange shapes, cones, and craters filled with water. Some geysers create pillars and columns of minerals around themselves.

Iceland has many geysers.

Soil and Erosion

What is soil?

Much of the Earth's surface is covered with soil. Soil is a mixture of mineral and organic (living) particles, dead plant and animal matter, air, and water. There are many kinds of soil, each formed slightly differently.

Could life exist without soil?

Life as we know it depends on soil. Most plants grow in soil, taking food from it. Animals in turn eat plants. Microbes (microscopic living things) in soil break down dead matter, which decays and so releases nutrients back into the soil.

The two layers of soil are topsoil and subsoil. Soils differ in the size of the particles they contain. Loamy soil, with a mixture of big and small particles, is best for growing crops.

Topsoil

Subsoil

Bedrock

Sandy soil

Clay soil

Loamy soil

How is soil made?

The mineral particles in soil are tiny bits of rock, worn small or "weathered" by rain, frost, wind, and sun. Chemical action, when water dissolves minerals, also helps make soil. Soil forms slowly. Warm, moist conditions are best for making soil.

How does soil become dust?

Soil that has never been cultivated is called virgin soil. Plowing makes soil more fertile for a while, as tiny creatures in the soil become more active and break down dead plant matter more rapidly. However, if the same crops are continually planted year after year, all the nutrients in the soil may be used up. The soil no longer sticks together. It falls apart and becomes like dust. A strong wind may then blow the dusty soil away leaving only the infertile subsoil or even bare rock.

How thick is soil?

Gardeners often talk of topsoil, meaning the uppermost layer of soil in which they grow their plants. The topsoil in most temperate (mild) regions of the Earth is up to 10 inches thick. Underneath is the subsoil, and beneath that is rock.

How do rivers and glaciers make soil?

Rivers carry mineral particles along with them. When a river changes course it leaves behind deposits of the minerals. These form alluvial soils. Material that was carried along by glaciers and then deposited when the glacier stopped or melted forms drift soils.

What makes some soils more fertile than others?

A fertile soil is rich in humus—a fine organic matter made by microbes, or soil bacteria, as they break down dead plants and animal waste. Soil microbes work best in warm, airy soil, where there is plenty of leaf mold or grass. The right amounts of minerals and water are needed to create fertile soil. Too much water washes nutrients from the soil. Too much evaporation (drying of water) can bring salts to the surface, making the soil less fertile and reducing the number and types of plants it can support.

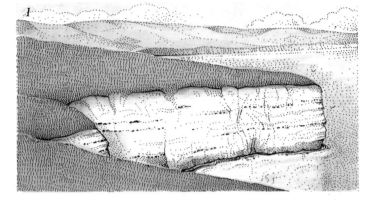

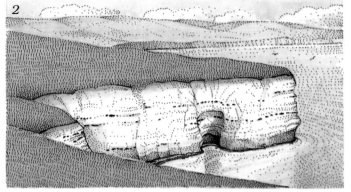

Rocky headlands are gradually eroded by the sea into arches and stacks of rock.

What is erosion?

Erosion is the wearing away of rocks and soil by wind, water, ice, and frost. It can happen quickly in a few years, or very slowly over thousands of years. The word erosion means "gnawing away." Erosion happens all the time. It can be done by glaciers, by the Sun's warmth, or by the scouring action of wind, rain, rivers, and ocean waves. Erosion alters landscapes, reshaping the Earth's surface.

Can farming cause erosion?

A large, plowed field can become dusty if left unplanted in dry weather. Winds may blow away the topsoil. Trees and hedges can act as windbreaks, protecting the field from the wind.

What are chestnut brown soils?

Grassland soils are brown because they are rich in humus (the decayed remains of plant and animal matter). Soils with plenty of humus are usually dark in color.

Can the sun crack rocks?

In hot deserts it is very hot by day and very cold by night because there are no clouds to act as a blanket and keep the ground warm. Rocks heat up during the day and expand (grow bigger). As they cool at night they contract (shrink). If this happens quickly, the rocks may break apart.

Will ice crack rocks too?

When water freezes, it expands. This is why frozen water pipes sometimes burst. Water in crevices in rocks also expands when it freezes. The pressure of the ice expanding can widen a crack and split off chunks of rock.

How much damage can a raindrop do?

You hardly feel a raindrop hitting your hand. But in a heavy downpour, millions of raindrops hit the ground in a short time. In regions that have most of their rainfall in one short season, heavy rain can damage the soil. The raindrops smash into the soil and break it up, washing it away into streams and rivers.

How does grazing destroy some soils?

Grazing animals such as goats can eat every blade of grass if too many are allowed to roam over one stretch of land. In dry soils animals will nibble away the roots that bind the soil together. Without plants the bare soil is easily blown away by the wind.

Why do wise farmers never plow up and down hills?

Flooding after heavy rain can do as much damage to soil as a storm wind. Water rushes over bare fields, taking with it the precious topsoil. On hilly land, if a farmer plows up and down the slope, instead of across it, the furrows left by the plow act like ditches. Water rushing down the ditches washes away topsoil and leaves deep channels.

Farmers avoid soil erosion on hillsides by planting crops in strips between grass or clover, to slow the flow of rainwater down the slope.

How do farmers prevent erosion?

Planting trees and shrubs checks erosion by binding the loose soil. Sowing grasses is another way to stop erosion. The grass helps build up new organic matter which binds together the soil crumbs and so prevents them from being blown away.

What keeps soil fertile?

Farmers use manure and fertilizers to restore nutrients to the soil. Nutrients can be conserved by planting grass for a season to let the soil rest between crops. Rotation of crops means growing different crops in succession: such as wheat one year, potatoes the next, and clover the season after. It is a good way to keep the soil rich in nutrients.

The Glacier of the Angel in Canada. Glaciers are spectacular slow-moving masses of snow and ice, grinding their way downhill.

What is a glacier?

A glacier is a slow-moving "river" of ice. Glaciers are found in cold, snowy regions and in high mountains wherever more snow falls in winter than melts in summer. The snow and ice form a huge mass that creeps downhill.

What starts a glacier moving?

A mountain glacier usually begins in a high mountain basin. Snow fills up the basin and is packed into a huge mass of ice. The pressure becomes so great that the ice begins to move. It slides out of the basin and down the mountain valley under the force of gravity.

How fast can glaciers move?

The top of a glacier moves faster than its base. Most glaciers are slow-moving, covering less than one foot per day. The Quaraya glacier in Greenland races along at up to 80 feet per day and is probably the fastest glacier. However other glaciers may "sprint" for as much as 400 feet in one day. These sprinting sessions can last a year or so, then the glacier stops and "rests" for perhaps 100 years.

How do glaciers stop?

Some glaciers end in warm lowlands and simply melt. When a glacier reaches the sea in very cold regions, huge chunks of ice split off the tip to form floating icebergs.

How does a glacier flatten hills?

A glacier is like an enormous grinding tool, cutting slowly through the landscape. It scoops up rocks as it goes and smooths hills in its path. It piles up loose material into ridges called moraines. It gouges out the sides of valleys, making them U-shaped. Melting glaciers leave rocky boulders scattered around. Hollows made by glaciers fill with water after the glacier has melted to form lakes.

What are ice ages?

From time to time large parts of the Earth are covered with sheets of ice. These ice ages, or glacials, happen every few million years. We are now in a warmer period, or interglacial. The most recent ice age lasted until about 10,000 years ago. Much of northern North America and Europe was covered by an ice sheet up to 10,000 feet thick.

What made the fjords of Scandinavia?

Along the coast of Scandinavia there are deep sea inlets called fjords. These inlets were made by glaciers. A glacier always seeks the easiest path down a mountain, such as a river valley. The ice widens and deepens the valley. After the ice melts, water from the sea flows in to fill the valley. There are also fjords in Chile, Alaska, and New Zealand.

What is a crevasse?

The top surface of a glacier is hard and stiff. The ice beneath is always shifting, as the glacier slides downhill. The surface often splits, forming deep cracks called crevasses.

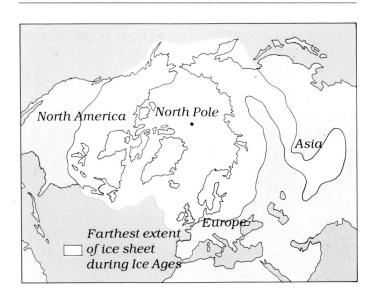

During the ice ages sheets of ice buried much of northern North America and Europe.

What is a cirque?

This is a bowl-shaped, steep-sided hollow eroded by a glacier. It is also known as a corrie. These hollows are often left flooded, as lakes, when the glacier retreats.

A glacier starts in a hollow basin called a cirque, high in a mountain. Rocks and soil pushed along by the glacier are piled up as moraines.

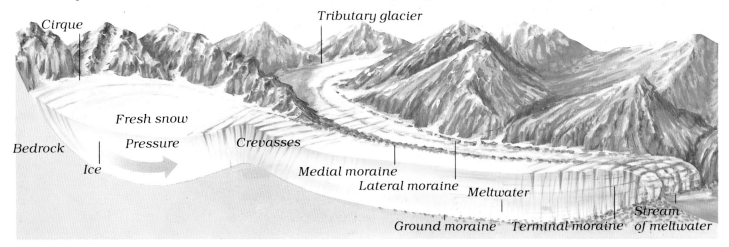

37

ATMOSPHERE and WEATHER

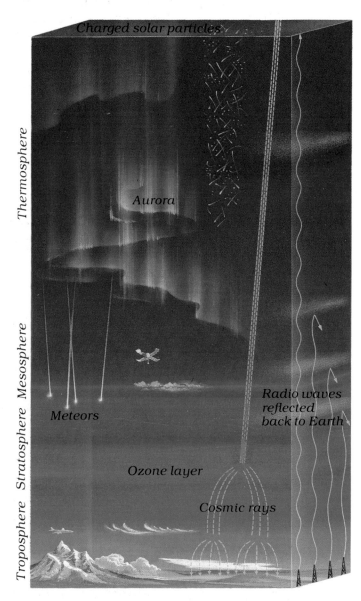

Thermosphere

Mesosphere

Stratosphere

Troposphere

Charged solar particles

Aurora

Meteors

Radio waves reflected back to Earth

Ozone layer

Cosmic rays

There are four main layers in the atmosphere. Within the thermosphere, the top layer, are two regions called the ionosphere and exosphere. Most weather happens in the troposphere.

What is the atmosphere?

The atmosphere is the layer of gas surrounding the Earth. The layer is surprisingly thin, yet without it there would be no life on Earth. When the Earth was young, the atmosphere consisted mainly of poisonous gases. Plants (which give off oxygen during photosynthesis) have enabled the atmosphere to support animal life.

Where does the atmosphere end?

The atmosphere starts at ground level. The higher the distance from the Earth's surface, the thinner it gets. At about 33,000 feet (about the height most airplanes fly), it is only one-third as dense as at sea level. Above 500 miles, the atmosphere merges into the near-emptiness of space.

What keeps the atmosphere from floating away from the Earth?

The Earth's gravity keeps the atmosphere from drifting off into space. The pull of gravity holds most of the gases in the atmosphere close to the ground. More than 75 percent of the atmosphere is squashed into the lowest layer, the troposphere.

How many layers does the atmosphere have?

There are four layers. At the boundaries between them there are differences of temperature. The *troposphere* is the lowest layer. It is between 6 and 10 miles thick. Above it is the *stratosphere*, about 20 miles thick. Higher still is the *mesosphere*, also about 20 miles thick. The uppermost layer is called the *thermosphere*. The thermosphere has two parts, the *ionosphere* and the *exosphere*.

What is air?

Air is a mixture of gases. The most plentiful gases in air are nitrogen (78 percent) and oxygen (21 percent). The remaining 1 percent is made up of water vapor and a mixture of other gases such as ozone, carbon dioxide, argon, and helium—all in very small amounts.

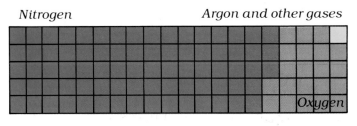

Nitrogen

Argon and other gases

Oxygen

Together, oxygen and nitrogen make up 99 percent of the air.

How much does the air weigh?

Air is much lighter than solids or liquids. But it has weight. At sea level a cubic foot of air weighs 1.25 ounces. The weight of all the air around the world is put at more than 5.7 trillion tons. Every one of us has almost a ton of air pressing down on us. We do not collapse under the weight because the same amount of air is pressing in on our bodies from all sides.

What is light?

Light is a form of energy, like heat. Natural light comes from the stars that shine because they have immense nuclear energy. The Sun, our star, gives off light. Light from the Sun takes just over eight minutes to travel to the Earth.

Why is the sky blue?

Light reaches the Earth from the Sun. Sunlight looks white but is actually a mixture of all the colors in the rainbow. When light rays from the Sun pass through the atmosphere, they are scattered by the tiny bits of dust and water in the air. The blue rays are scattered most and reach our eyes from all angles. We see more blue than any other color, and this makes the sky look blue.

At sunset dust particles in the atmosphere filter out all colors of light except red.

How was the ozone layer formed?

Millions of years ago some of the oxygen in the atmosphere drifted high into the upper levels. There it was changed by the Sun's radiation into ozone. The ozone formed a protective layer against the harmful ultraviolet rays from the Sun. Without it, animal life below could not have evolved.

Why should you never look directly at the Sun?

The Sun is a giant powerhouse, radiating vast amounts of heat and light. Even when screened by the Earth's atmosphere, its light is much too powerful for our eyes. Never look directly into the Sun, even when you are wearing sunglasses. The rays are bright enough to damage your eyes or even cause blindness.

Why are sunsets red?

At sunset the Sun is low in the sky and farther away from us as we look toward it. The light rays from the Sun have to pass through more layers of air to reach our eyes. This extra air filters out all the colors in the sunlight except red. Only the red rays come straight to our eyes, and so we see a red sunset.

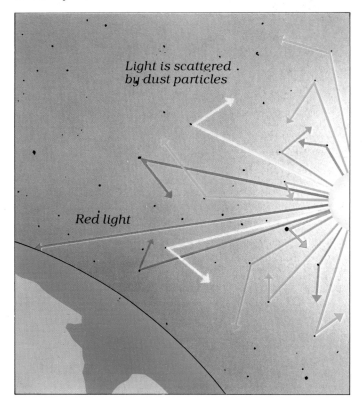

Light is scattered by dust particles

Red light

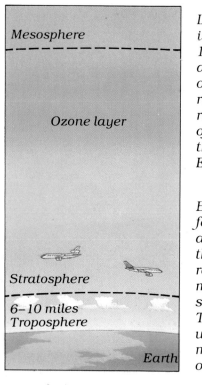

Left: The ozone layer is between 9 and 18 miles high in the atmosphere. The ozone forms a radiation shield, reducing the amount of ultraviolet rays that reach the Earth's surface.

Below: Ozone is formed in the upper atmosphere when the Sun's ultraviolet rays split oxygen molecules (O_2) into separate atoms. These combine with whole oxygen molecules to form ozone (O_3).

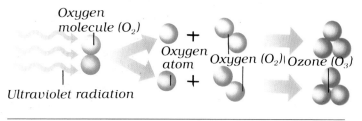

Where is the ozone layer?

Ozone is a form of oxygen. In the atmosphere, it forms when oxygen in the air reacts under the electrical influence of sunlight. Most ozone forms near the equator and is shifted by the winds around the Earth. The ozone layer is an invisible screen. The ozone filters out the harmful ultraviolet rays from the Sun.

How much ozone is there in the atmosphere?

The ozone in the atmosphere is very thinly spread out. If all the ozone were squashed down at sea level to cover the Earth, it would make a layer only one-eighth of an inch thick. Scientists have discovered that the ozone layer is thinner than it used to be. Some of the ozone has been destroyed by gases called CFCs, which were used in aerosols, refrigerators, and packaging materials.

Could we live in the thermosphere?

No human could live at this height; there is no air, and it is so hot our bodies would burn up. The thermosphere begins about 50 miles above the Earth's surface. At this height the atmosphere is very thin. The atmospheric pressure is only one-millionth of the pressure at ground level. Also, the thermosphere is completely exposed to the rays of the Sun.

Why do aircraft fly in the stratosphere?

The stratosphere is very dry and so almost cloud-less. Most of the Earth's weather takes place under-neath it. Aircraft in the stratosphere can therefore fly clear of storms, fog, or other weather problems.

What are the northern and southern lights?

The northern lights, or aurora borealis, are mar-velous displays of colored lights in the sky, like enormous laser shows. You can see them in or near the Arctic. The southern lights, or aurora australis, are seen in or near the Antarctic. The lights are caused by electrical particles from the Sun hitting the atmosphere and giving off bursts of light.

The northern lights seen in Alaska

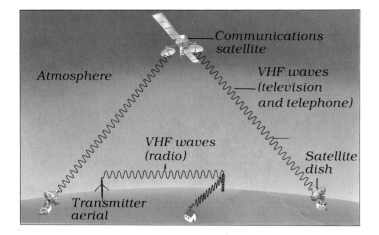

The ionosphere does not reflect very high frequency (VHF) radio waves, and satellites are needed to send these signals around the globe.

How does radio use the ionosphere?

When the Sun's radiation hits the atmosphere, it gives an electrical charge to some atoms and molecules in the air. These charged particles are called ions. The ions are mostly in the lower part of the thermosphere—the ionosphere. Low frequency radio waves bounce off these ions and back to Earth. This allows us to send some radio signals long distances without having to bounce them off space satellites.

Why do spacecraft heat up when they re-enter the atmosphere?

When a spacecraft returns to Earth from space, it moves very fast as the Earth's gravity pulls it toward the ground. As it enters the atmosphere, the spacecraft hits a thickening blanket of air. This causes friction, which makes the spacecraft glow red-hot. Heat shields made of heat-absorbing materials protect the craft from being scorched.

Why does sunlight darken the skin?

Sunlight contains ultraviolet rays. We cannot see them, but they are vital to health. They enable skin cells to make vitamin D. However, ultraviolet rays damage the outer layer of skin. The body reacts by making more of a brown pigment called melanin. This darkens the skin. The ozone layer shields us from most of the ultraviolet rays.

How hot does the atmosphere get?

The atmosphere acts as a heat shield, protecting life on Earth from the full power of the Sun's energy. The outer atmosphere is exposed to the full glare of the Sun, and the thin air there becomes very hot. During a solar storm, when bursts of extra hot energy shoot out from the Sun, the air 250 miles above the Earth is heated to 3,600°F.

Does it get colder the higher you go?

Anyone who has climbed a high mountain knows that you need warmer clothes near the top than at the bottom. The temperature falls by about 3.5°F for every 1,000 feet of altitude. The troposphere can get as cold as −112°F. Yet higher up, in the stratosphere, it gets warmer, rising to about 28°F. The mesosphere is cold, down to −165°F, but in the thermosphere, 250 miles above the Earth, temperatures can reach 3,600°F.

Where is the air over the equator colder than the North Pole?

Within the troposphere, the coldest region is where the air rises highest—over the equator. It can be as cold as −112°F. Over the North Pole, where the air rises less high, it can be 30 degrees warmer.

When a spacecraft such as the Shuttle re-enters the Earth's atmosphere, friction causes the craft to get very hot. Shields made of heat-absorbing materials protect the craft and its crew from being scorched to cinders.

What do we mean by climate?

Climate is the average, or usual, weather of a place over a period of many years. Weather can change from day to day, but climate stays the same.

Why are some climates hotter than others?

The Sun has the greatest effect on climate. Its rays heat the land, the air, and the oceans. Land near the equator receives more heat from the Sun's rays because the Sun is directly overhead. These lands usually have a hotter climate than countries farther away from the equator. The Poles get less heat from the Sun because the Sun's rays have farther to travel through the atmosphere. The polar regions therefore have very cold climates.

Why is it warmer at noon than early morning?

The Sun's warming effect is less strong in early morning and late evening. This is because its rays strike the ground at a shallow angle. At noon the Sun is high overhead. Its rays hit the ground more directly and give out more warmth.

What are climatic zones?

The Earth has five major climatic zones. They are polar (cold); cold forest (cold winters); temperate (mild winters); desert (dry); and tropical rainy (warm and moist). There are variations of climate in each zone, because other factors such as height above sea level and distance from the sea play a big part in controlling climate.

What are weather highs and lows?

These are the two main air-pressure systems that control weather. Highs are formed when cool, heavy air sinks. The outward spiral of air from a high pressure area is called an anticyclone. The spiral of winds moves clockwise in the Northern Hemisphere and counterclockwise in the Southern Hemisphere. Anticyclones bring clear skies, with long dry spells in summer and frost, icy winds, and bitter cold in winter. Lows are formed when warm air rises, reducing air pressure close to the ground. Air flows in to replace the rising warm air, creating an inward spiral. Winds blow counterclockwise around a low in the Northern Hemisphere and clockwise in the Southern Hemisphere. A low-pressure system is known as a cyclone or depression and often brings unsettled weather with winds, storms and rain.

In an anticyclone (left), air spirals outward from a high-pressure area. The reverse happens in a cyclone or depression (right).

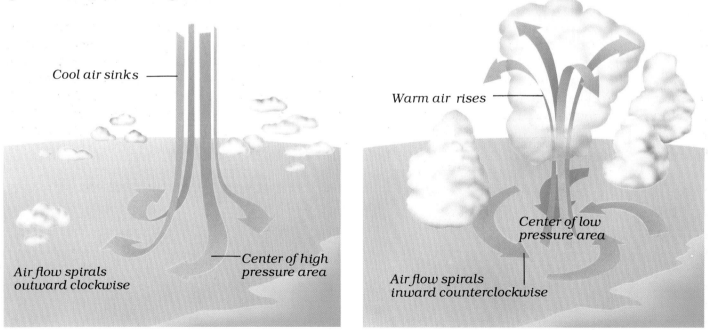

Cool air sinks

Air flow spirals outward clockwise

Center of high pressure area

Warm air rises

Center of low pressure area

Air flow spirals inward counterclockwise

The water cycle

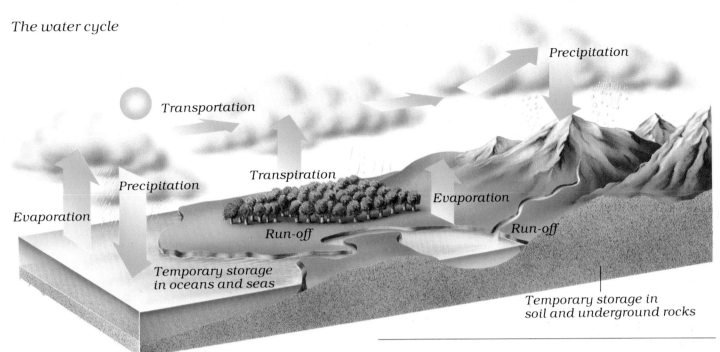

Water evaporates from the ocean. Some falls as rain and some is blown inland. Trees and other plants give off moisture. Clouds formed high above mountains release rain and snow, feeding rivers which return the water to the ocean.

What makes rain?

Water from the oceans, lakes, rivers, and plants is evaporated by the Sun's heat to form water vapor. This vapor, or gas, is held in the air. Air rises when warm, when forced to rise over mountains, or when heavier cold air pushes underneath it. As the warm, moisture-laden air rises, it cools. The water vapor condenses back into water droplets, which mass together to form clouds. As the air rises, more vapor turns to water. The clouds grow bigger. When the water droplets are too big for the air to carry, they fall as rain.

Why do clouds change shape?

Look at clouds in the sky, and you will see they have many different shapes. Some clouds are billowing white masses, some are delicate bonelike traces, others are huge stone gray slabs. Clouds change shape all the time, as bits of them evaporate when they meet drier air. The wind also changes the shapes of clouds.

What is sleet?

Sleet is a mixture of snow and rain, or partly melted snow which reaches the ground.

What does a psychrometer measure?

A psychrometer measures the humidity of the air. It is an instrument used by meteorologists.

What does a thundercloud look like?

Storm clouds often form on warm summer days. As the ground warms up and surface water is evaporated, small clouds form in the sky. These clouds may grow into towering cumulus clouds that rise higher and higher. They may build into a dark mass of cumulonimbus cloud. This huge cloud can be 60,000 feet high. Often such clouds bring a thunderstorm.

Why are there often clouds above mountains?

Clouds form when moist air rises and cools. This happens when a mass of warm air blows over mountains. The air is forced to rise, and it cools as it does so. This cooling makes the water vapor in the air condense as water droplets. Clouds then build up over the mountains.

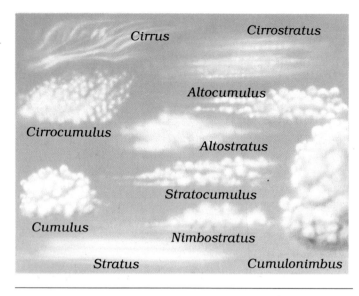

Different types of clouds bring different weather. Puffy cumulus clouds often mean fine weather. Low stratus clouds bring rain.

How can scientists make rain?

People all around the world have traditional beliefs in rain gods. Rain dances and other magical ceremonies are performed to bring the rain needed to water crops. Scientists can make rain by "seeding" rain clouds with chemicals dropped from an airplane. The method works best on clouds already quite heavy with water vapor. Making rain clouds in a clear blue sky is much more difficult.

What are the highest clouds in the sky?

High clouds include cirrus, cirrostratus, and cirrocumulus. These clouds are formed mainly of ice crystals. Cirrus clouds are wispy clouds and can form at heights up to 35,000 feet. The rare nacreous clouds can be over 66,000 feet high.

Which is the wettest place in the world?

Tutunendo in Colombia, South America, has the highest average yearly rainfall—465 inches. Imagine six tall men standing on one another's shoulders: that's how deep 465 inches of water would be! Cherrapunji in India holds the record for the most rain in one month (360 inches) and the most rain in a year—an astounding 1,058 inches in 1860–1861.

Where does it rain nearly every day?

People living near the equator, on the coast, or on islands are most likely to need their umbrellas every day. Rain normally falls every day in parts of West Africa and the Amazon River basin in South America.

Where does the most snow fall?

In one year (1971–1972) Paradise, Mount Rainier, in Washington State, had over 103 feet of snow. This makes it the snowiest place in the world. The record for the most snow in one snowstorm is 16 feet. This was in 1959 at Mount Shasta in California.

Why do some lands have monsoons?

A monsoon is a wind. It blows from sea to land in summer and from land to sea in winter. In hot lands near the equator the air heats up in summer and rises. Cool air carrying moisture from the ocean is drawn inland to take the place of the rising warm air. The cool winds bring rain which is often torrential. In India the monsoon season lasts from three to four months.

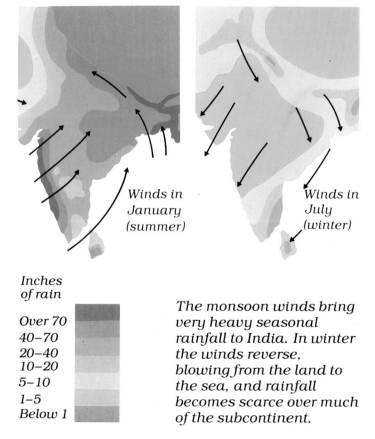

Winds in January (summer)

Winds in July (winter)

Inches of rain

Over 70
40–70
20–40
10–20
5–10
1–5
Below 1

The monsoon winds bring very heavy seasonal rainfall to India. In winter the winds reverse, blowing from the land to the sea, and rainfall becomes scarce over much of the subcontinent.

What makes a rainbow?

Sunlight is a mixture of colors. When the Sun's rays pass through falling raindrops, the raindrops act like tiny mirrors or glass prisms. They bend and scatter the light into all its colors. We see a rainbow when the Sun is behind us and the rain in front of us. You can make your own rainbow with a water sprinkler or hose on a bright, sunny day.

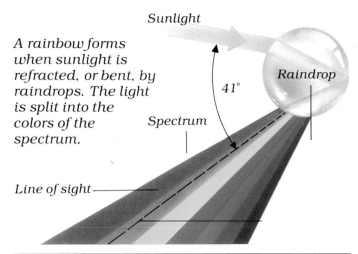

A rainbow forms when sunlight is refracted, or bent, by raindrops. The light is split into the colors of the spectrum.

Where is the hottest place on Earth?

The hottest places are near the equator, which receives the Sun's strongest rays. In 1922 a temperature of 136°F in the shade was recorded in the Libyan desert in North Africa. Another very hot place is Death Valley in California, where a high temperature of 134°F was measured in 1913.

Which is colder: the North or South Pole?

The South Pole gets colder than the North Pole ever does. The coldest spot on Earth is at the Vostok base in Antarctica, not far from the South Pole. In July 1983 the temperature there fell to −128.6°F.

Where does the Sun never shine?

Even on a cloudy day, the Sun does not disappear. People above the clouds in an aircraft can see bright sunlight. However, at the Poles there are long periods of permanent night during the polar winter. At the South Pole there is no Sun for 182 days of the year. The North Pole gets a little more Sun. There the Sun is absent for only 176 days.

What is frost?

The layer of white frost that covers the ground on cold mornings is made by moisture in the air. On cold nights the water vapor in the air freezes when it meets the cold ground. A thin layer of ice crystals forms to make frost.

Which contains more water: snow or rain?

Polar explorers sometimes melted snow to make drinking water. It took a lot of snow to fill a kettle because snow has less water in it than rain. To make as much as one cup of rainwater you would need to melt ten cups of dry snow.

Are snow and hail made in the same way?

Snow and hail are both frozen water, but they are formed in different ways. In very cold air, water vapor turns to ice crystals. The crystals cling together to make a snowflake. If raindrops freeze, hailstones form. Hailstones form inside thunderclouds, in which air is swept up and down violently. The hailstones grow bigger with extra layers of ice when they swirl up into the freezing cold at cloud-tops.

How big can hailstones be?

Hailstones can be much bigger than snowflakes. A big hailstone can be larger than a tennis ball and weigh nearly 2 pounds. Huge hailstones are said to have killed 90 people during a storm in Bangladesh in 1986. The more a hailstone is swept up and down inside a cloud, the icier and heavier it gets. Finally it gets so heavy that the air can no longer carry it upward, and it falls to Earth.

Precipitation falls as rain, sleet, or snow, depending on air temperature.

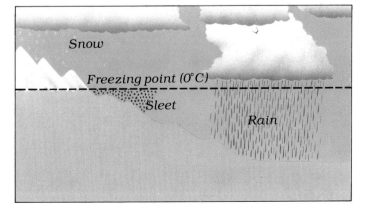

Dew drops form on leaves during the night.

What is dew?

Dew forms on clear, still nights. As the temperature falls, water vapor in the air cools into water droplets. In the morning, we see the water as beads of moisture sparkling on cars, plants, and spiders' webs. Frozen dew becomes frost.

Where is the ground always frozen?

In the coldest parts of the world the ground is frozen all year round. This frozen layer is called permafrost. Permafrost more than 4,000 feet thick has been measured in Siberia, Russia.

What causes fog?

Fog is a cloud that reaches the ground. Like clouds, fog is made of tiny water droplets floating in the air. The cooler the air becomes, the less water it can hold as water vapor. The vapor condenses and forms water droplets. The air becomes foggy.

Why does the Sun clear fog?

Morning mist (thin fog) is soon cleared by the warmth of the Sun. As the Sun heats up the air, the air is able to hold more moisture. The water droplets in the fog turn to invisible water vapor, and the air becomes clear once more.

What is humidity?

Humidity is the amount of water vapor in the air. The warmer the air is, the more water vapor it can hold. Saturated air holds the maximum possible amount of water vapor. Relative humidity is the amount of water vapor in the air compared to the amount the air can hold at its saturation level. Relative humidity is highest (nearly 100 percent) over oceans and lowest over deserts (about 10 percent).

What causes lightning?

Lightning is a huge electric spark. During a thunderstorm, very large electric charges build up inside clouds and on the ground. The charges build up until a flash of lightning shoots through the air between them. Lightning can flash from the cloud to the ground, or between two clouds.

How often does lightning hit the ground?

At any one moment there are 1,500 or more thunderstorms around the world. Each one is producing lightning, and every minute about 6,000 lightning flashes hit the ground.

Advection fog forms when warm, moist air moves over cool ground or when cold air moves over warm water. Frontal fog forms where a cold air mass meets a warm one. Radiation fog forms at night as the air at ground level cools. Upslope fog forms as moist air cools when forced uphill.

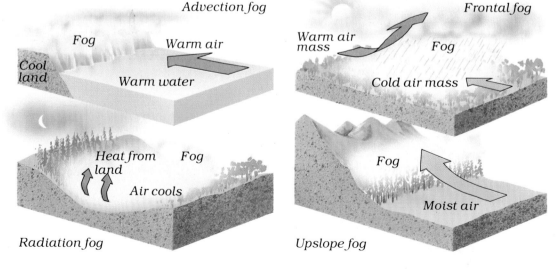

Advection fog

Fog
Warm air
Cool land
Warm water

Frontal fog

Warm air mass
Fog
Cold air mass

Heat from land
Fog
Air cools

Radiation fog

Fog
Moist air

Upslope fog

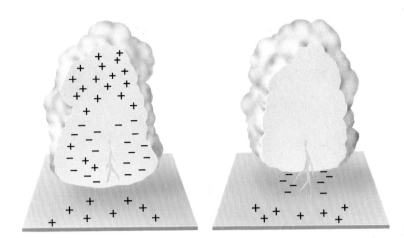

Lightning is a sequence of flashes. First a leader stroke zigzags to the ground. The main flash then surges upward. Other flashes may follow in quick succession.

How fast does lightning flash?

A lightning flash begins on the downward "leader stroke," which seeks out the easiest path to Earth. It travels at up to nearly 1,000 miles per second. The return stroke, upward, is much quicker—as fast as 89,000 miles per second, or almost half the speed of light.

Does lightning ever strike the same place twice?

Lightning can kill people and damage buildings. An old saying maintains that "lightning never strikes twice." In fact, it does. It can hit the same tall building (if it is protected by a lightning conductor) hundreds of times a year. A park ranger in Virginia has survived being hit by lightning seven times!

Why should you not seek shelter under a tree during a thunderstorm?

The downward stroke of a lightning flash seeks out the highest object to find the easiest path to the ground. Tall or lone trees, especially on hills, are dangerous places to shelter. Holding a metal object (such as a golf club or umbrella) during a thunderstorm can also increase the risk of being hit by lightning since metal conducts electricity.

What is thunder?

People once believed thunder was the sound of the gods' anger. In fact, thunder is the sound air makes as it expands when it is warmed by the heat of a flash of lightning.

Can you tell how close a thunderstorm is?

The nearer you are to a thunderstorm, the closer together are the lightning flash and the thunderclap. Count the seconds between them. Divide the number by five and you have an estimate of how many miles away the thunderstorm is.

Why does thunder always follow lightning?

A flash of lightning heats up the air around it. The heated air expands, producing sound waves that we hear as a thunderclap. We see the lightning flash almost as it happens. But the sound of the thunderclap travels much more slowly, and we hear it a few seconds later.

Thunder is the sound made as air is heated very rapidly by lightning. The sound waves travel much more slowly than the light from the lightning flash. So we hear the thunderclap after we see the lightning.

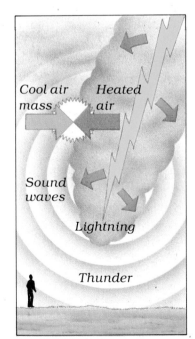

Cool air mass   Heated air

Sound waves

Lightning

Thunder

Why do winds blow?

As the Sun heats the air it causes winds. Warm air expands, making it lighter than cold air. Because it is lighter it rises, and cool air flows in to take its place. The Sun's heat is greatest at the equator. The warm air here rises, cools as it does so, and moves outward. Cooler air moves in underneath it, to create the winds of the world.

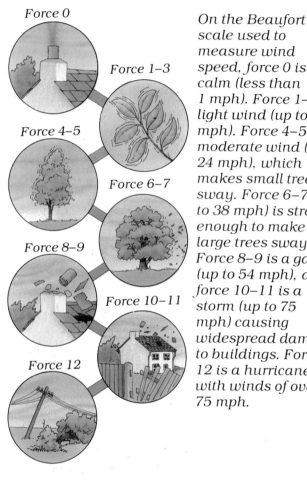

On the Beaufort scale used to measure wind speed, force 0 is calm (less than 1 mph). Force 1–3 is a light wind (up to 12 mph). Force 4–5 is a moderate wind (up to 24 mph), which makes small trees sway. Force 6–7 (up to 38 mph) is strong enough to make large trees sway. Force 8–9 is a gale (up to 54 mph), and force 10–11 is a storm (up to 75 mph) causing widespread damage to buildings. Force 12 is a hurricane, with winds of over 75 mph.

What is a gale?

Wind is moving air. Winds moving at different speeds are called by different names. A slow wind is a breeze. A fast wind is a gale. A scale of wind speeds was worked out in 1805 by a British admiral, Sir Francis Beaufort. On the Beaufort scale the force of a wind is shown by numbers from 0 to 12. Zero shows that the air is calm; force five is strong enough to make a small tree sway; force nine is a gale that is strong enough to damage the roofs of houses.

How fast do winds blow?

The fastest wind speed on record is 230 miles an hour. This was measured on Mount Washington in New Hampshire in 1934. Winds in a tornado can be even faster, around 250 miles an hour.

What are trade winds?

In the early days of sea exploration and trading, sailors needed the wind to cross the oceans. This is how the trade winds got their name. These winds blow steadily toward the equator and are known as "prevailing" winds. The spin of the Earth pushes the winds so that they blow roughly east to west. Sailing ships took advantage of these prevailing winds when making long trading voyages.

Where is the eye of a hurricane?

A hurricane is a violent tropical storm. On the Beaufort scale of wind speed a hurricane is force 12. In a hurricane, winds spiral around very rapidly. The twisting mass of cloud can be over 300 miles in diameter. At the center of the hurricane is the eye. It is only 9 miles in diameter, and here the air is calm.

Why do hurricanes begin over the ocean?

Hurricanes form over the ocean near the equator, where the air is very warm and moist. The warm air rises rapidly, and cooler air rushes in beneath it. The air begins to move in a spiral, like a giant whirling top. Hurricanes form in the Atlantic Ocean. Similar storms in the Pacific Ocean are called typhoons. Indian Ocean hurricanes are called cyclones.

The winds in a hurricane spiral around the eye.

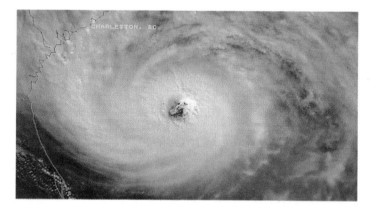

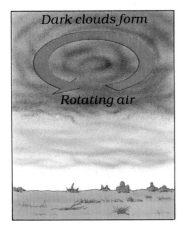

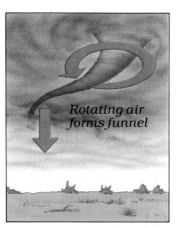

A tornado is a violent twisting wind. The dark clouds form a downward-twisting funnel which eventually touches the ground. The strong updraft inside a tornado can hurl houses and trees several hundred yards.

What is a tornado?

A tornado is a storm wind similar to a hurricane. It forms over the land when huge masses of clouds meet. The clouds whirl around each other. Then they join to create an enormous funnel. The tip of the funnel spins down to the ground, where it sucks up everything in its path. Tornadoes in the central United States cause great damage. They rip across the country at 20 to 30 miles an hour and can be heard 20 miles away.

What happens when winds hit a mountain?

When winds blow against mountains, the air is forced higher and cools. Clouds form. Some high mountains are often hidden by clouds. Most rain and snow falls on the windward side (the side facing the wind). The leeward, or far, side is drier.

These instruments are used to measure weather conditions. Anemometers measure wind speed, psychrometers measure humidity, and the barograph records changing air pressure.

What is a chinook?

A chinook is a warm, dry wind that blows down the eastern slopes of the Rocky Mountains in North America. It can bring sudden warm weather, melting snow quickly. The European Alps also have similar winds, called foehn winds.

What causes sea breezes?

Near the coast, winds often blow from the sea to the land. In summer the Sun's rays heat up the land more quickly than the sea. The air above the land heats up and rises. Heavier cold air from the sea moves in underneath it, causing a cool sea breeze.

What is a weather front?

A front is where most changes in weather occur. It develops when a mass of cold air meets a mass of warm air. Cold fronts cause sudden changes in weather, such as strong winds, rain, or snow. Warm fronts usually bring more gradual changes.

What are the high- and low-pressures of weather forecasts?

Air pressure is the force of the atmosphere pushing down on the Earth's surface. Warm air weighs less than cool air. Warm air therefore forms a low-pressure area, or low. These areas usually have cloudy skies. High-pressure areas, or highs, have cooler air and usually have clearer skies.

Who forecasts the weather?

Scientists who forecast the weather are called meteorologists. They collect information from more than 3,500 weather stations around the world, from weather ships and buoys at sea, from planes and balloons in the skies, and from space satellites.

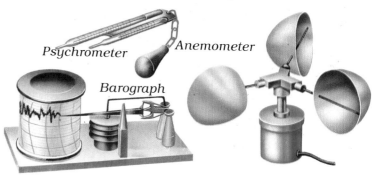

OCEANS, RIVERS, and LAKES

The Pacific and Atlantic are the biggest oceans.

How much of the Earth is ocean?

Almost 71 percent of the Earth is covered by ocean. That is 217 million square miles. The world's great oceans contain 97 percent of all the water on Earth. The world can be seen as one mass of ocean with the continents as islands in between.

How were the oceans formed?

Scientists do not know for certain when or how the oceans were formed. Some think that the water came from rocks inside the Earth as they cooled. Others believe that the water fell as rain from thick clouds that surrounded the newly formed Earth; for hundreds of years, as the Earth and the clouds cooled, rain fell and filled up the oceans.

Do all the oceans meet?

The oceans are part of one vast body of water. The three great oceans—the Pacific, Atlantic, and Indian—all meet around Antarctica in the Antarctic Ocean. The Atlantic and Pacific also meet in the Arctic Ocean.

How long does water take to travel around the world?

Some oceanographers (scientists who study the oceans) have worked out that it would take 5,000 years for one particle of water to move through all the oceans of the world.

What is a current?

A current is a stream of water moving through the ocean. There are surface currents and deep water currents. Great surface currents carry warm water away from the equator. The water cools and mixes with colder water as it gets farther away from the heat of the equator. When the current turns toward the equator again, its waters are cold. Offshore currents are caused by the movement of the tides. But the much larger currents circling in the oceans are caused by winds.

Which way do currents go?

As a result of the Earth's rotation (spinning), the great ocean currents move in clockwise circles in the Northern Hemisphere and counterclockwise in the Southern Hemisphere. Deeper currents often flow below surface currents replacing the water pushed away by winds. Surface and bottom currents move in opposite directions.

What are gyres?

The movements of the main ocean currents create six vast, swirling water patterns called gyres. There are two gyres in the Atlantic, two in the Indian Ocean, and two in the Pacific. Gyres transport heat around the oceans, which often affects the climate of nearby land areas.

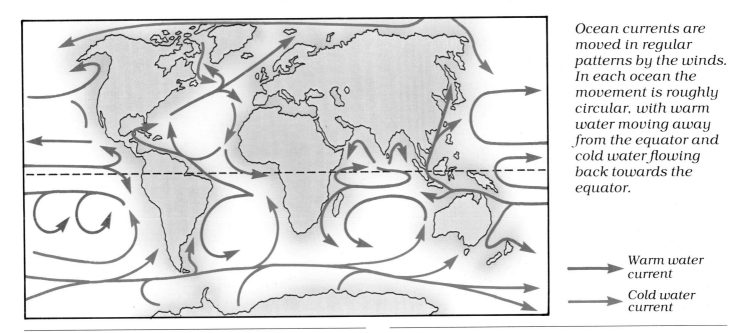

Ocean currents are moved in regular patterns by the winds. In each ocean the movement is roughly circular, with warm water moving away from the equator and cold water flowing back towards the equator.

→ Warm water current

→ Cold water current

How do currents affect the land?

Ocean currents have an important effect on land temperature. The North Atlantic Drift, or Gulf Stream, is a warm Atlantic current. Its waters flow northeastward, warming the coast of western Europe. This current gives France, Britain, Norway, and Iceland warmer winters than most other places so far north. The waters of the Gulf Stream are up to 18°F warmer than the waters around it. The Peru or Humboldt Current is a cold current in the Pacific. Along the west coast of Peru in South America, the water is 14°F colder than other Pacific waters at the same latitude.

How does warm Pacific water end up on the shores of Britain?

Part of the Gulf Stream's warmth actually comes from the Pacific Ocean. A huge warm current, the Agulhas Current, flows from the Pacific east into the Indian Ocean and around the southern tip of Africa into the Atlantic. It then flows north to warm the waters that end up washing the shores of northwest Europe, keeping Britain largely ice-free in winter.

Although waves travel toward the shore, the water does not move forward. The wave travels over the surface, and the water particles move in a circular orbit as the wave passes.

How fast does the Gulf Stream travel?

The water in the main ocean gyres moves at about 6 miles a day. Narrow warm water currents like the Gulf Stream move faster, as much as 96 miles a day.

How big can waves be?

Storm waves, driven by high winds, often rise 40 feet or more in an open sea. The highest sea wave seen from a ship and officially recorded was 112 feet high, during a hurricane in 1933. The biggest wave measured by instruments was 86 feet high in 1972 in the North Atlantic.

What makes waves?

If you watch a ball floating in the sea, the waves seem to roll underneath it. Each wave is made up of water particles moving in a circle. The wind pushes the wave upward, forming a crest. Then gravity pulls it down again, into a trough.

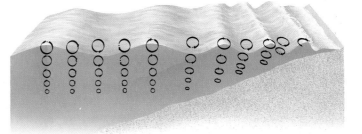

How hot is the hottest seawater?

The sea has invisible underwater boundaries, formed by layers of pressure and temperature. The hottest seawater measures 95°F (nearly human blood temperature) and is in the Persian Gulf. Much hotter water (759°F) has been found bubbling up from the seabed. The great pressure of water around it keeps this water from turning to steam.

Which waves cause the greatest damage?

Giant ocean waves called *tsunamis* (the name is Japanese) are made by movements of the sea floor, such as an earthquake. The wave crests can be hundreds of miles apart. They travel very fast, up to 600 miles an hour. In the open ocean the waves are not big enough to disturb a fishing boat. Yet when they enter shallow water, the waves rear up to 250 feet or more, smashing everything in their path and causing terrible damage.

Why is seawater salty?

The saltiness of the sea comes from minerals. Minerals are washed from the land into the sea by rivers, which dissolve minerals from the rocks over which they flow. The most plentiful mineral in seawater is sodium chloride, or common salt.

Why is the Dead Sea the saltiest sea?

The Dead Sea is in the Middle East. It is surrounded by hot desert. The Sun's heat evaporates a great deal of the seawater, leaving behind the salt it contained. The water that remains therefore becomes even saltier. The Dead Sea is about nine times as salty as the great oceans and is more buoyant because of this. Bathers can float in it with no effort.

Why do the tides rise and fall?

Ocean tides rise (flood) and fall (ebb) about twice every 24 hours. Tides are caused by the gravitational pull of the Sun and Moon on the Earth. They tug at the Earth's waters, pulling the oceans toward them. The land is pulled too, but water moves more easily, creating a bulge or giant wave. As the Earth spins on its axis, this tidal bulge travels around the Earth, causing the tides.

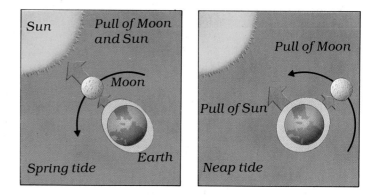

The highest tides (spring tides) occur when both the Sun and Moon are pulling in the same direction. The lowest tides are neap tides, when the Sun and Moon pull against one another.

What is an upwelling?

An upsurge of cold water. When winds blowing offshore push away warmer surface water, colder water from deeper in the ocean rises. This cold water is rich in food for fishes, so such upwellings create good fishing grounds.

What are spring tides?

Spring tides are very high tides. They occur when the gravitational pull of the Sun and Moon are combined. This happens when the Sun and Moon are pulling together on the same side of the Earth. When the Sun and Moon pull against one another, there are low neap tides.

Which place has the biggest tides?

Tide size is the vertical distance between high tide and low tide. Record tides occur in the Bay of Fundy, which lies between Nova Scotia and New Brunswick, Canada. Here there is a 50-foot difference between the high-tide mark and the low-water mark during the spring tides. The shape of the coast and the sea floor, and prevailing winds can exaggerate extreme tides.

Where is the greatest ocean current?

The biggest current is the Circumpolar Current in the Antarctic Ocean. It is 1,200 miles wide at its greatest width. In the Pacific Ocean, water from the Antarctic moves north as far as Japan, where it meets cold water spreading south from the Arctic.

Oceans and Seas

Which is the biggest ocean?

The Pacific Ocean is by far the biggest ocean on Earth. It covers an area of about 70 million square miles. That is more than the Atlantic and Indian oceans put together. About 45 percent of all the world's seawater is in the Pacific.

How many oceans are there?

The three great oceans are the Pacific, Atlantic, and Indian. There are two smaller oceans, the Arctic and Antarctic, although some geographers say that they are part of the great oceans and not separate. Seas are smaller bodies of salt water. Many seas are in fact joined to the great oceans. The Mediterranean Sea, for example, is joined to the Atlantic Ocean.

The Pacific is by far the biggest ocean, larger than the Atlantic and Indian oceans together. Most smaller seas are part of one of these three great oceans.

Where is the deepest point in the oceans?

The deepest point in the oceans is the bottom of a deep trench called the Mariana Trench in the Pacific. Measurements of the Trench have varied from 36,203 to 35,815 feet below the surface.

What is a bay?

A bay is a wide inlet of sea, partly enclosed by water. The biggest bay in the world is the Bay of Bengal in south Asia, which has a surface area of 868,800 square miles. The longest bay shoreline in the world is Hudson Bay in Canada. If you were to walk around it, you would walk 7,200 miles!

What makes a whirlpool whirl?

A whirlpool is a mass of water spinning around, as if it were being sucked down a giant drain. Whirlpools are created in several ways. A current meeting rocks or tides can cause a whirlpool. Two currents meeting can also make a whirlpool, as can winds pushing against the tidal flow. A famous whirlpool is the Maelstrom, off the coast of Norway.

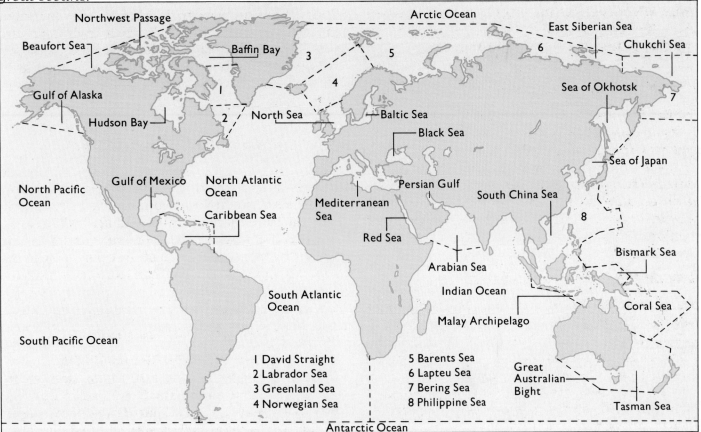

1 David Straight
2 Labrador Sea
3 Greenland Sea
4 Norwegian Sea
5 Barents Sea
6 Lapteu Sea
7 Bering Sea
8 Philippine Sea

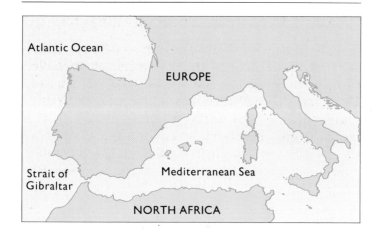

The Mediterranean Sea is the world's largest inland sea.

What is a strait?

A strait is a narrow channel of water linking two oceans or seas. The Strait of Gibraltar connects the Atlantic Ocean and the Mediterranean Sea. It is about 30 miles long and only 8 miles wide at its narrowest point. It separates Europe (Spain) and Africa (Morocco).

What makes the Sargasso Sea unusual?

The Sargasso Sea is a large area of the western Atlantic Ocean. It is unusual because of the large amount of seaweed growing in it and floating on the surface. Crabs, shrimps, and fish live among and beneath the weeds. The waters of the Sargasso are unusually blue in color, very warm and salty, and extremely clear. The Sargasso has slow-moving currents but is surrounded by much faster currents, including the Gulf Stream.

Why did sailors fear the Sargasso Sea?

Sailors exploring the Atlantic from the late 1400s brought back strange tales of the Sargasso. They told of a place of mystery and doom, where sea monsters lurked amongst the tangled weed and wrecked ships rotted. In fact, the seaweed poses no danger to ships. It floats in scattered masses and is not thick enough to trap a vessel. Nor are there any sea monsters!

Where is Cape Horn?

A cape is a point of land jutting out into the sea. Cape Horn is at the tip of South America. The seas here are stormy, and in the early seafaring days, ships often faced a rough passage as they "rounded the Horn" to sail from the Atlantic into the Pacific.

What is El Niño?

Every few years the water in the eastern Pacific Ocean gets warmer. This warm water pushes away the normally cold water from the coasts of Peru and Ecuador. The warming of the sea is called "El Niño," Spanish for "the child," because it often happens near Christmas. El Niño has an effect on climate far beyond South America. It causes more rain and floods in the eastern Pacific, but less rain and often drought in places in the western Pacific.

Is the Black Sea black?

The Black Sea lies between Europe and Asia. It is often foggy in winter, making the water look dark. That may be why it got its name. It can also be suddenly stormy. The ancient Romans must have found the Black Sea more welcoming. They called it Pontus Euxinus, Latin which means "friendly sea."

Where is the White Sea?

The White Sea is in Russia and is part of the Arctic Ocean. It is linked with the Barents Sea by a long narrow strait known as the "Throat." The coast of the White Sea is broken by a number of deep gulfs or inlets which are frozen over for half the year.

The Sargasso Sea is part of the western Atlantic Ocean and is not really a sea at all.

The Ocean Floor

Where is the continental shelf?

In most places, land does not stop suddenly at the coast. It slopes gently away beneath the sea to a depth of about 600 feet. This undersea land is called the continental shelf. Its shallow waters stretch out to sea for hundreds of miles in some areas. At the outer edge of the shelf the steeper continental slope begins, leading down to the deep ocean floor—the abyss.

What is the ocean bottom like?

The deep basins of the ocean floor are formed from heavy rock called basalt. Layers of mud overlie the deep oceanic trenches and level parts of the ocean floor. Some of the muds are filled with the remains of dead plants and animals. Such muds are called oozes. They are hundreds of feet deep in places.

Are there mountains under the ocean?

Yes. The landscape beneath the oceans is varied, like that above them. Great mountain ranges rise from the bottom. The Mid-Atlantic Ridge runs for 9,600 miles along the middle of the Atlantic Ocean. Some of its peaks form islands, including the Azores. Many undersea mountains are volcanoes, which also form islands in the ocean. The Hawaiian Islands were made by volcanoes rising from the sea floor.

Is there any gold in the ocean?

All the natural elements found on Earth are in seawater. Among the metals dissolved in it are millions of tons of gold and silver. Also present are magnesium, sulfur, potassium, and calcium. The relative amounts of common salt and other elements in seawater are about the same in all the oceans. In future, the sea may supply us with minerals that have become scarce on land.

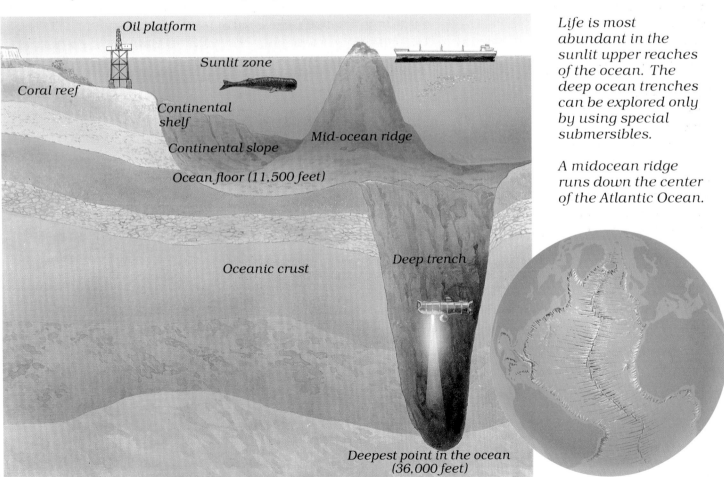

Oil platform

Sunlit zone

Coral reef

Continental shelf

Continental slope

Mid-ocean ridge

Ocean floor (11,500 feet)

Oceanic crust

Deep trench

Deepest point in the ocean (36,000 feet)

Life is most abundant in the sunlit upper reaches of the ocean. The deep ocean trenches can be explored only by using special submersibles.

A midocean ridge runs down the center of the Atlantic Ocean.

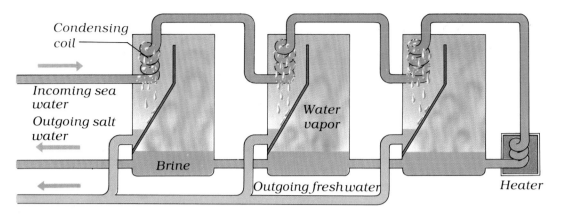

Seawater can be made fresh by distillation. The salt water is boiled to produce fresh water vapor. This is directed over a condenser, where it cools back into a liquid.

Can you drink seawater?

Seawater is about seven times more salty than water that is safe to drink. Anybody who drank only seawater would die. Their body would dry out as it tried to rid itself of all the salt.

How can seawater be made drinkable?

Many ways to remove the salt from seawater (desalinate it) have been tried. The oldest and simplest way is to distill it. This can be done by boiling seawater in a container and leading off the steam into a cold bottle. The steam leaves the salt behind in the container so that fresh water condenses in the bottle. Modern methods of desalinating water on a large scale are expensive and produce relatively little fresh water. The world's desalination plants produce over a billion gallons of fresh water each day—a small fraction of the world's demand.

Reflected sound wave — Sonar wave

Shipwreck

What made the deepest dive of all time?

Ordinary submarines are not strong enough to withstand the immense pressure of water thousands of feet down. To reach such depths scientists must use a special craft called a bathyscaphe. In 1960 the bathyscaphe *Trieste* descended into the Mariana Trench, about 36,000 feet down.

Can you see easily in the ocean depths?

There is no sunlight in the ocean below about 5,000 feet. Beyond that depth it is pitch-dark and very cold. The Sun's rays cannot reach the ocean bottom. To see the strange creatures that live there, special cameras and strong lights are needed.

When were the ocean depths first studied?

The *Challenger* expedition of 1872 was the first to explore the ocean depths. British scientists gathered information from the ocean for three and a half years. This was the beginning of oceanography, the scientific study of the sea.

How do scientists explore the seabed?

We can explore the seabed in several ways: by echo sounding from surface ships, by drilling into the sea floor, and by diving into the ocean. To explore deeper down, scientists use submarines.

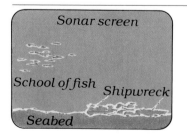

Sonar screen

School of fish   Shipwreck

Seabed

Sonar screens use sound waves reflected back from underwater objects to build up a sound-picture of the sea floor.

Rivers

Where does a river begin?

River water comes from rain, from lakes and springs, and from melting ice and snow. A river begins as a trickling stream. Its starting point is called the source and is often on a mountain.

Can rivers flow uphill?

No. All rivers start on high ground and flow down-hill, under the pull of the Earth's gravity. A river may form from several streams coming together. These streams are its headwaters. As they flow downhill, more water finds its way into the streams, making them larger.

What are tributaries?

Tributaries are rivers that flow into a larger river. A great river such as the Amazon may have many tributaries, some of which are big rivers themselves. The river and its tributaries form a river system.

How does a river grow?

A river begins its journey as a small bubbling rivulet or rill. The rill grows and flows down a wider, deeper channel as a brook. The brook tumbles downhill, getting wider and deeper. Brooks join to form streams, and eventually streams come together to create a river.

The muddy waters of the Amazon join the blue-black waters of the Rio Negro in northwest Brazil.

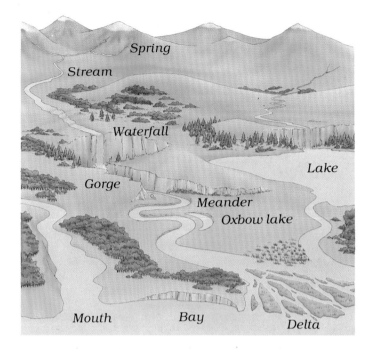

Over thousands of years a river carves out a valley as it flows toward the sea. It begins as a tiny mountain stream, flowing rapidly downhill. It may cut its way over a waterfall. Finally it loops lazily through flatter land toward the sea, where it deposits mud to form a great delta.

Where is a river's basin?

A river system drains a large area of land, and this area is known as its drainage basin. The biggest river basin in the world is that of the Amazon River in South America. The Amazon basin covers an area of 2.7 million square miles, which is nearly as big as Australia.

Where do rivers end?

A river flows into a larger river, into a lake, or into the sea. The end of a river is called its mouth. An estuary is where the fresh water of the river mixes with the salt water of the sea.

Do rivers flow faster as they near the sea?

A young river tumbles down the slopes of a moun-tain. It cuts a narrow channel for itself. The slope of the channel is usually steepest near the river's source. Nearer the sea, the channel of a river is much wider and the slope more gentle, so the water flows more slowly.

The Nile Delta is one of the biggest in the world. Huge amounts of mud and other deposits are carried by the river to its mouth.

What is a delta?

A delta forms where a river meets the sea. The river flows more slowly and deposits mud, sand, and even boulders that it has carried. This material piles up, forming new land. The delta is shaped like a triangle. It gets its name from the letter Δ (delta) in the Greek alphabet.

Why are some deltas so big?

The delta of the Nile River covers about 9,600 square miles. The delta of the Mississippi is even bigger, about 14,000 square miles. Both of these rivers carry huge amounts of mud to the sea. Near their mouths, tides are weak, so the mud is not washed away. It piles up, forcing the river to cut new channels to reach the sea. The delta is a network of channels, constantly shifting and changing.

Why don't rivers run a straight course?

Canals, waterways dug across land, usually run in straight lines. A river bends and wanders along its course, seeking the easiest path to the sea. Where it meets an obstruction, such as a hill or boulder, it curves around it.

Why do rivers meander?

A slow river is easily turned away from its course. So as a river nears the sea, moving slowly through flat country, it may often take a winding course. Slight bends become big bends, because the water on the outer curve flows faster than that on the inside. The faster current wears away the bank on one side, and the river moves in meanders or snaky curves. Meanders get bigger and bigger. Sometimes meanders become U-shaped bends.

What is an oxbow?

The meanders in a river can become so big that an oxbow is formed. Eventually the bends cut themselves off from the river. The river flows on in a new course, leaving behind an oxbow lake.

Where is a river's floodplain?

The middle or lower stretch of a river's course is often through flat land. On both sides of the river the land may be so low that flooding often occurs after heavy rains or after snow on the mountains has melted in spring. This area is known as the river's floodplain. Some rivers have floodplains hundreds of miles wide.

River meanders change shape as the water current erodes the outside of the bend and sand and mud are deposited on the inside.

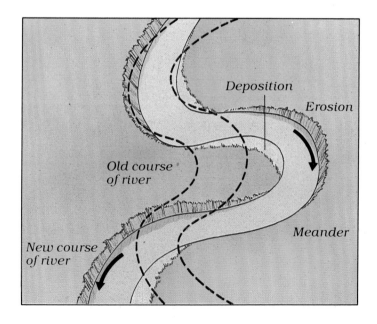

How are canyons made?

A canyon is a deep valley cut by a river. A narrow canyon with steep rocky walls is a ravine or gorge. The biggest canyon in the world is the Grand Canyon in Arizona. It was cut by the waters of the Colorado River over millions of years. Parts of the Grand Canyon are almost a mile deep.

Which is the longest river?

The Nile in Africa and the Amazon in South America are close rivals for the title of the world's longest river. Most measurements make the Nile longest, at 4,145 miles, slightly more than the Amazon, at 4,000 miles.

Which river carries the most water?

The Amazon carries more water than any other river. At its mouth it pours an average of 4 million cubic feet of water every second into the Atlantic Ocean. The mouth of the Amazon is over 90 miles wide.

Where is the Zaire River?

Formerly known as the Congo, this African river is the fifth longest river in the world, at 2,900 miles. Only the Amazon carries more water.

The Grand Canyon in Arizona is 277 miles long and up to 18 miles across.

How far out to sea can a river's waters flow?

The Amazon spills out so much water that a ship approaching the coast will meet the river's waters over 180 miles out to sea. From an aircraft, the river's waters look like a huge mud-colored patch in the ocean.

How old is our drinking water?

Rivers are part of the Earth's water recycling system. The water we drink is at least 3 billion years old. That is when the first rains fell on Earth. Since then, the same water has been recycled over and over again.

Which is the muddiest river?

The Huang He or Yellow River in China is muddier than any other river. Each year about 2 billion tons of soil are washed down the Yellow River. With so much mud you could build a wall 10 feet high and 10 feet thick that would stretch around the world 27 times!

How do rivers recycle water?

All the world's water is constantly in circulation. Water from the oceans is drawn up as water vapor by the Sun's warmth. The vapor is blown over land by winds. Clouds form and the water vapor falls as rain and snow. Rivers collect water from the ground and return it to the ocean for the cycle to start all over again.

Can rivers flow under the sea?

Rivers are known to flow underground, even beneath deserts. They also flow under the sea. A river with a water flow 1,000 times greater than the Mississippi River has been traced flowing beneath the surface 300 feet down in the Pacific Ocean.

Can a river flow backward?

A stronger movement of water against it, such as an incoming sea tide, can reverse the flow of a river, making it flow backward. This creates a wave known as a tidal bore that rushes upstream. In Canada the St. John River flows over a waterfall before entering the Bay of Fundy, which has the world's highest tides. At high tide the incoming sea pushes the river water back over the waterfall.

How big can a bore be?

A high ocean tide pushes a bore, or tidal wave, upstream. A famous bore in England rushes up the Severn River. It is about 7 feet high and travels at about 12 miles per hour. One Chinese river has a tidal bore 23 feet high.

How are swamps formed?

When a slow-moving river moves through lowlands, it may form a swamp—an area of wetland. A swamp has more woody plants (trees and shrubs) than a marsh. Close to the sea, salt and fresh water often mingle and mix in a swamp. Swampland often floods.

Are marshes water-covered all the time?

No, but a swamp is always waterlogged. A marsh is only water-covered part of the time (by the incoming tide, for example).

The formation of a waterfall

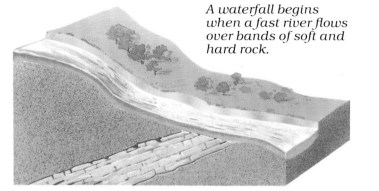

A waterfall begins when a fast river flows over bands of soft and hard rock.

The soft rock is worn away more quickly than the hard rock, and a ledge forms.

Over thousands of years more rock is worn away, and the waterfall gets bigger.

How is a waterfall made?

Waterfalls are found in the upper part of a river's course. They are made in places where the river crosses a layer of hard rock. The hard rock is worn away more slowly than the softer rock downstream, forming a "step" that gradually gets deeper. Water plunges over the step, creating a waterfall.

Where is the highest waterfall?

At the Angel Falls, or Cherún Merú, in Venezuela, South America, the water falls 2,648 feet in a single drop. This is the world's highest waterfall. The total drop of this waterfall is 3,212 feet.

Which waterfall pours the most water?

The biggest waterfalls (the ones with the most water) are called cataracts. The Boyoma Falls in Zaire have an average flow of 600,000 cubic feet of water every second. Other falls exceed this at times when their rivers are full, with flows of up to 1.8 million cubic feet of water a second.

Where was the greatest waterfall of all time?

In prehistoric times, enormous waterfalls were caused by movements of the Earth. Over five million years ago, what is now the Mediterranean Sea was dry land. It filled with water from the Atlantic Ocean, pouring through the gap between Europe and Africa—the Strait of Gibraltar. This would have created a gigantic waterfall, about 2,500 feet high and pouring water at a rate at least 25 times greater than the largest waterfall on Earth today.

How can a waterfall move backward?

At the edge of a waterfall are layers of rock, hard on top, often softer underneath. The water wears away the soft rock and undercuts the jutting hard rock, which weakens and breaks off. The waterfall thus moves slowly upstream.

The Angel Falls in Venezuela

How many falls are there at Niagara?

The Niagara River forms part of the boundary between the United States and Canada. At the Niagara Falls, water pours over a cliff. An island named Goat Island divides the river, making two falls: the American Falls and the Canadian or Horseshoe Falls. The Canadian Falls are 2,500 feet wide, and the American Falls are 1,000 feet wide.

What are rapids?

Rapids are stretches of fast-flowing, rough river water. The water tumbles and rushes around large boulders. The boulders are made of hard rock, left behind after softer surrounding rocks have been worn away by the river.

White-water rafting over the rapids of a river is a thrilling experience.

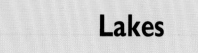

Lakes

How are lakes formed?

Most lakes are in areas once covered by glaciers. A glacier cuts deep valleys as it moves. Earth and boulders carried along by the glacier are deposited when it melts, making a dam. Melting ice from the glacier fills the valley to make a lake. Huge lakes such as the Caspian Sea and the Great Lakes were formed by movements of the Earth's crust. Other lakes are formed in the craters of extinct volcanoes or when a river changes its course.

Is the Great Salt Lake really salty?

The Great Salt Lake is an inland sea in northwest Utah. It expands and shrinks from time to time. During the summer it gets smaller because more evaporation takes place. It is fed by freshwater streams, yet it is more salty than the ocean. This is because the waters of the lake do not drain away but dry up in the heat of the summer.

The Great Lakes of North America

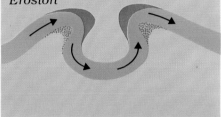

Silt deposit

Erosion

New course of river

Oxbow lake

The formation of an oxbow lake

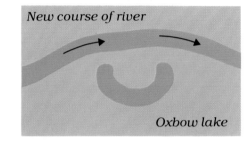

Where are the Great Lakes?

The Great Lakes of North America form the largest group of freshwater lakes in the world. The biggest is Lake Superior, with an area of 31,700 square miles. It is also the deepest, with a maximum depth of 1,333 feet. There are four other Great Lakes: Huron, Michigan, Erie, and Ontario.

Which is the smallest Great Lake?

Ontario is the smallest of the Great Lakes (7,550 square miles in area). The shallowest of the Great Lakes is Erie (maximum depth 210 feet).

What is the world's largest lake?

The Caspian Sea on the borders of Russia, Azerbaijan, Turkmenistan, Kazakhstan, and Iran is the biggest body of inland water in the world. It has an area of 143,630 square miles. It is 750 miles long. The Caspian's waters are salty, so it is sometimes thought of as a sea rather than a lake. A canal links the Caspian with the Black Sea.

Where is Lake Tanganyika?

This lake in east-central Africa is the longest fresh-water lake in the world, at 420 miles. It is the second deepest, 4,708 feet at its deepest point.

Which is the deepest lake?

Lake Baikal in Siberia (Russia) is the deepest lake in the world at 5,315 feet, and a maximum crevice depth of 6,402 feet. It contains more than 20 percent of the world's unfrozen fresh water.

Which is the world's oldest lake?

Baikal is also the world's oldest lake, with an estimated age of 25 million years. Because it is so old, it has immensely thick sediments on its bottom. The next oldest lake, Tanganyika, is only 2 million years old.

Which are the world's greatest artificial lakes?

By damming rivers, engineers have created vast artificial lakes. Among the largest are Lake Nasser in Egypt (1,550 square miles) and Lake Volta in Ghana (3,240 square miles).

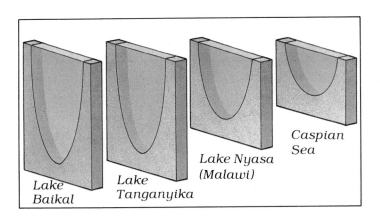

The four deepest lakes in the world. Baikal is the oldest as well as the deepest lake.

Where are there lochs and loughs?

Lakes in Scotland are called lochs, and lakes in Ireland are called loughs. Lough Neagh in Ireland is the largest lake in the British Isles. The largest loch in Scotland is Loch Lomond.

The Aswan High Dam on the Nile created the artificial Lake Nasser.

Where is the highest navigable lake?

The highest lake on which motor boats travel is Lake Titicaca in South America (part in Peru and part in Bolivia). This lake is 12,507 feet above sea level. There are higher lakes in the Himalayas, but these are often filled with ice for much of the year.

Which great lake is crossed by the equator?

Lake Victoria is Africa's largest lake and the second largest freshwater lake in the world, with an area of 26,828 square miles. The great lake is the main source of the Nile River, the world's longest river. It is bounded by Uganda, Kenya, and Tanzania and is crossed by the equator.

How big is Lake Superior?

The biggest freshwater lake in the world, Lake Superior covers 31,700 square miles. It is 338 miles long and over 150 miles wide.

Why was Lake Kariba in danger of becoming choked with weeds?

The waterweed Salvinia auriculata is probably the most difficult weed to clear away. It was first spotted in Lake Kariba in Africa in 1959, and in only four years it had covered an area of more than 400 square miles.

LANDSCAPES

What is a desert?

A desert is a region that has less than 10 inches of rain a year. Deserts cover between one-seventh and one-eighth of the Earth's land. Hot deserts lie between 20° and 30° either side of the equator. There are cold deserts too, which are permanently covered by snow and ice.

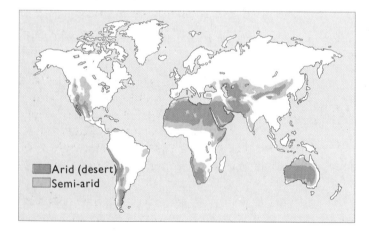

Arid (desert)
Semi-arid

About one-seventh of the Earth's land is desert.

Why are some deserts near the sea?

Cool ocean currents can help form a desert. If cool ocean water meets warm air from the land, clouds and fog form. But winds blowing from land to sea keep this moisture from reaching the land. Such conditions keep the coastal deserts dry in Namibia (southern Africa) and Peru (South America).

On poorly drained land, salt builds up in the soil as the water table (the level of water held in the rocks) rises. The salt kills plant life, aiding the process of desertification.

How do warm winds keep deserts dry?

Over many deserts warm winds absorb almost all the moisture from the land, drying it up. Warm air from the equator moves north and south, rises, cools, and releases moisture (as rain). By the time it reaches the desert zone, the air is dry, especially if it has crossed a mountain. It takes up any moisture from the ground in the desert.

Do deserts ever have rain?

Deserts receive little rainfall, but few areas in the desert get no rain at all. One very dry desert is the Atacama Desert of Chile in South America. Until 1971 no rain had fallen there for at least 100 years. Some deserts go without rain for several years but then have a brief downpour.

Have deserts always been deserts?

Deserts may once have been green with plants. Animals would have grazed and hunted across them. A change in climate may have caused the rains to cease. Without rain, the land would have dried up and the plants died. Without plants to bind and nourish the soil, the land would have become barren. Most of the animals would have moved away or died too. Then only desert would have remained.

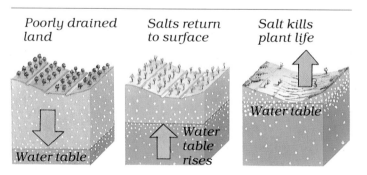

Poorly drained land   *Salts return to surface*   *Salt kills plant life*

Water table

Water table rises

Water table

Can people create deserts?

People living on the edge of deserts are in a delicately balanced environment. If farmers keep too many animals, such as goats (which nibble plants down to the roots), and cut down trees (whose roots bind the thin soil), they can speed up the spread of deserts.

What is sand?

Sand is made up of tiny mineral grains, the biggest of which are only one-twelfth of an inch across. Sand is rock broken apart and crumbled by weathering. The most common mineral in sand is quartz.

Are all deserts sandy?

No, only about one-fifth of hot deserts are covered with sand. The rest are rocky, stony, scrubby, or icy.

How big is the Australian Desert?

After the Sahara, the next biggest desert is the Australian Desert. This is actually several deserts with a total area of 600,000 square miles—less than one-sixth the size of the Sahara.

Are all deserts hot?

Most deserts are found in hot countries, but not all. The Gobi desert in central Asia is hot in summer but cold in winter. The Antarctic is a frozen desert.

A sandy desert. Deserts are not all sand, like giant beaches. Most are rocky or stony.

What is an oasis?

An oasis is a patch of green in the desert. Plants grow because there is water from a well or an underground spring. The water is trapped deep down in the rocks beneath the desert. Palm trees and vegetables can be grown by people living at an oasis. Some oases support quite large towns.

A desert oasis

Which continent has the most deserts?

Asia, the biggest continent, has the most deserts. They include the world's third largest desert—the Arabian, as well as the Gobi, the Taklimakan in China, the Kara Kum of Turkmenistan, and the Thar of India and Pakistan.

Is the Sahara growing or shrinking?

In the early 1980s the Sahara was getting bigger, as sands spread southward. Recent satellite pictures seem to show that the desert then began to retreat, getting smaller. In 1987, for example, the desert moved 32 miles south, but in 1988 it retreated 58 miles north.

What is a mirage?

A traveler in the desert may see what looks like a pool of water and hurry toward it—to find only more dry sand. The "pool" was a mirage. In hot deserts the air near the ground becomes very hot. It expands and becomes less dense. This makes light bend in unusual ways. Instead of traveling in a straight line through the air, the light follows a curved line. The "pool" is a reflection of light from the sky bent by the layer of hot air near the ground. This is why mirages are most often seen in hot countries.

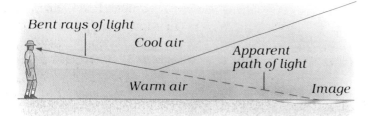

A mirage is seen when light from the sky is bent by the layer of hot air above the ground.

What is a barchan?

This is a crescent-shaped sand dune. The tip of the crescent points downwind. The gentler slope of the dune is on the windward side.

When was the Sahara ice-covered?

The Sahara Desert was probably ice-covered about 450 million years ago. The Sahara region was then near the South Pole.

Can the desert make waves?

Loose sand is easily driven along by wind. It piles up in wave-like hummocks called dunes. Wind blows the sand grains up the windward slope of a dune. The grains roll over its crest and down the steep far side. This constant movement of sand up and over the dune makes it roll across the desert, like a wave across an ocean.

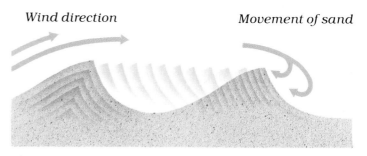

Wind direction   *Movement of sand*

Sand dunes are driven by the wind. The sand grains roll up one side of the dune, over the crest, and down the other side.

How high can sand dunes grow?

In the Algerian part of the Sahara Desert there are sand dunes as high as 1,400 feet.

What is an erg?

Most of the Sahara Desert is gravelly or rocky. About one-tenth of the desert is wind-blown sand. This sand forms large sand-seas, known as ergs. The biggest is the Grand Erg Oriental, between Algeria and Tunisia. It covers about 207,200 square miles.

What is the "Empty Quarter"?

The world's largest area of sand dunes is Rub' al-Khali, or "the Empty Quarter," in Egypt's Eastern Desert. It covers about 260,000 square miles and contains sand mountains 800 feet high.

Which is the world's biggest desert?

The Sahara Desert in northern Africa is easily the biggest desert in the world. Look at a map of Africa, and you will see how much of northern Africa is covered by the Sahara. It fills an area of 3.5 million square miles—bigger than the whole of Australia and not much smaller than Europe.

Seashore

Which came first: sea or beach?

The sea constantly pounds the rocks of the coast, wearing them down. As the fragments of rock become worn, they break up into smaller particles. These build up to form muddy, sandy, and shingle beaches. Beaches build up on sheltered stretches of coast, such as in bays.

Where is the splash zone?

Various animals and plants make their homes on different parts of the beach. The different areas are called zones. The littoral zone lies between high- and low-water marks (high and low tide). Below the low-water mark is the sublittoral zone, permanently under water. Just above the high-water mark is the splash zone, which is splashed by waves but only covered by an unusually high tide.

What makes mangrove swamps?

Mangrove swamps are found along tropical coasts. The mangrove tree has a tangle of stiltlike roots reaching down into the mud, and these create the swamp. The mass of roots traps silt (mud particles) which piles up in the water, and this silt slowly forms new land. Mangroves grow in shallow, slow-moving water.

A mangrove swamp. Each tree sends down a tangle of roots into the mud. The roots trap silt, which gradually forms new land.

Tough grasses help to stabilize sand dunes.

On which side of a sand dune do most plants grow?

Some plants, such as marram grass, can root even in sand piled up by the wind on the dry shore. The sheltered side of a dune (out of the wind) has more plants than the exposed windward side.

How can you tell beach sand from desert sand?

Using a microscope, you could see that grains of desert sand are more rounded than beach sand. Desert sand grains are always being blown around by the wind. They rub against one another and this makes them all about the same size. Beach sand is treated less roughly, because it is cushioned by water, so its grains are more varied in size.

What are strand lines?

As waves roll up a beach, they carry with them all kinds of debris. At high tide this is left stranded on the beach in a line which shows the high-tide mark. New strand lines are left every day because the tidal range varies from day to day.

What are salt marshes?

Salt marshes are stretches of flat mud along the shore that from time to time are flooded by the incoming sea. Salt marshes often form near river estuaries and behind sandbars, where the sea has piled up mud. Small ponds and tidal creeks are features of salt marshes.

What is a lagoon?

A lagoon is a stretch of salt water, separated from the open sea by a narrow strip of land. When large waves break offshore, a sandbank begins to pile up. Another smaller sandbank forms closer to the land as sand is pushed up by smaller waves. In time the large offshore sandbank rises above the water. Between it and the smaller sandbank there is an area of quiet water, a lagoon.

Why do rock pools grow more salty?

Rock pools are like miniature aquariums on the seashore. Fish, crabs, and other sea creatures can live in them after the tide has ebbed. However, a shallow pool will warm up quickly when exposed to the sun. The heat evaporates water from the pool, which becomes steadily saltier unless refilled by rain or another incoming tide.

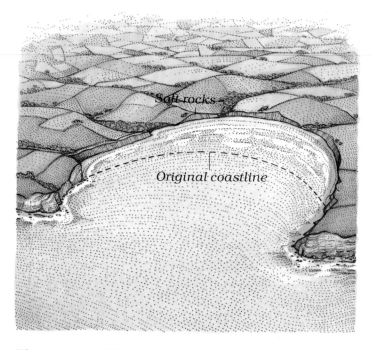

The action of the waves erodes away soft rocks, forming bays along the coast.

How does the sea create bays and headlands?

Ocean waves constantly wear away the rocks of sea cliffs. Soft rocks such as chalk wear away more quickly than hard rocks. The sea acts on weaknesses in the cliff, opening up cracks. As the crack widens, part of the cliff may collapse. The sea carves out bays from weak rocks. Harder rocks are left standing as headlands or as arches and stacks surrounded by water.

Fjords are narrow coastal inlets formed by glaciers. The coast of Norway is broken by many fjords, some reaching far inland.

Islands

How are islands made?

Some islands are chunks of land that became separated from continents. The British Isles, for example, were once joined to Europe. Others are volcanoes that have risen up above the sea. The islands of Japan are volcanic islands.

Where is the world's biggest coral reef?

The Great Barrier Reef lies off the coast of northeastern Australia. It is over 1,200 miles long and is the world's longest reef. It is famous for its brilliantly colored corals and wonderful variety of sea animals. Most of the reef is a national park.

How are coral reefs formed?

The tiny coral animals of warm seas create some of the oceans' most spectacular sights—coral reefs. The limestone remains of the animals build up walls and ridges of coral. Plants and animals move in to colonize the coral reef. Coral reefs are found only in tropical oceans because the coral animals cannot live in cold water.

What is an archipelago?

An archipelago is a group or chain of islands. The world's biggest archipelago is 3,300 miles long and has more than 13,000 islands. It forms the Southeast Asian nation of Indonesia.

Coral reefs form in shallow tropical waters. The corals form many beautiful colors and shapes.

Is coral dead or alive?

Coral is a kind of limestone found in warm, shallow seas. Coral is made by tiny animals called coral polyps. These animals build limestone shells around themselves. Thousands of polyps live together in colonies, or groups. When the animals die, their limestone skeletons remain.

What is an atoll?

An atoll is a doughnut-shaped coral island. First, a fringing reef of coral forms on the outer rim of a volcanic island that is slowly sinking into the ocean floor. In time, mud and sand pile up on top of the reef, and plants begin to grow. The central volcanic island has by now sunk completely under the water. Only the circular reef remains. There are many coral atolls in the Pacific Ocean.

An atoll in the Pacific Ocean. The circular coral reef encloses a lagoon.

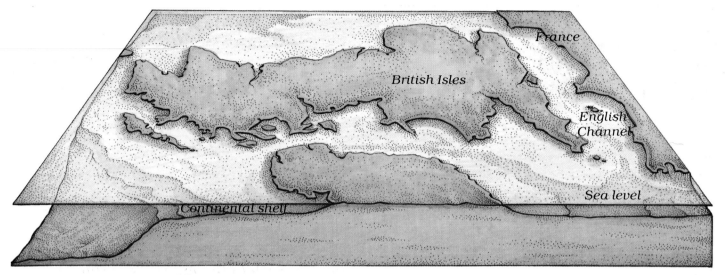

France

British Isles

English Channel

Sea level

Continental shelf

What are island hot spots?

Many island groups in the Pacific Ocean (such as the Hawaiian Islands) are not scattered haphazardly but are arranged in a straight line. They are all volcanic in origin, and those at one end are always much younger than those at the other end. This is because these islands were formed over a hot spot, a small but very active spot of volcanic activity in the Earth's mantle. Hot magma from deep within the Earth is forced up through the crustal plate and forms an island. The crustal plate drifts away, and a new island forms over the hot spot. The first island is carried farther away by the moving plate, and a chain of new islands is formed.

The formation of an atoll

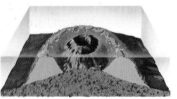

A coral reef forms around the volcanic island.

In time the island sinks below the water.

Only a coral reef, or atoll, remains above the water.

As the glaciers melted at the end of the Ice Age, the seas rose, filling the English Channel and separating Britain from the rest of Europe.

What is a continental island?

Continental islands are areas of land that were once connected to a continent. For example, the British Isles were part of mainland Europe when the sea level was lower. The two main islands lie on the European continental shelf. They were separated from the rest of Europe when the sea rose and the continental shelf was covered. Some continental islands are fragments of land that split off from the main landmass when the continents began to drift apart 200 million years ago. Greenland is the largest continental island.

Which is the world's biggest island?

Australia is usually called a continental landmass (part of Australasia or Oceania). The largest island is therefore Greenland, which has an area of about 840,000 square miles. Greenland may in fact be several islands joined and covered by one vast sheet of ice.

What is a barrier island?

This is an island that is made as sand, silt, and gravel build up along a shoreline. The wind and the ocean waves pile up the sand into ridges and dunes. This happens on gently sloping shores. An example of a barrier island is Hatteras Island in North Carolina.

Polar Regions

What is it like at the South Pole?

The polar regions of the Arctic and the Antarctic are vast frozen deserts. At the South Pole there is no life of any kind. Snow and ice lie hundreds of feet thick, burying the land far beneath. For half the year there is permanent darkness.

How wide is the Arctic Circle?

The Arctic Circle is a line on the map at latitude 66° 30′ north, marking a distance of 1,630 miles from the North Pole. The area within this circle is mostly ocean. The Arctic also includes parts of northern Europe, Asia, and North America, as well as thousands of islands.

How big is the Antarctic?

The Antarctic covers about 5.4 million square miles—an area bigger than either Europe or Australia. However, the land of Antarctica is actually smaller than Australia. Its huge size is due to the enormous mass of ice covering it. Antarctica contains almost nine-tenths of all the ice on Earth. But for much of its long geological history, it has been ice-free, and may be again sometime in the future.

The Antarctic is ice-covered and treeless. Only in its oceans does life abound.

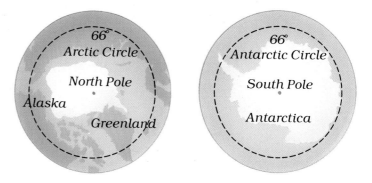

Within the polar circles lie some of the coldest and most barren areas of the Earth.

Where is a fly the biggest land animal?

Although both the Arctic and Antarctic are bitterly cold, much of the Arctic has no snow in summer. Plants with flowers and berries grow in some places. Caribou and musk-oxen graze on the plants. The Antarctic, on the other hand, has only a few mosses and lichens and just two flowering plants. Its largest land animal is a small wingless fly. However, while the Antarctic land has almost no life, the seas around are rich in animals, such as fish, seals, and whales, including the mighty blue whale.

How thick is the Antarctic ice?

The thickest ice in the Antarctic is 15,700 feet deep. That is more than ten times the height of the world's tallest skyscraper.

Can you climb up the North Pole?

The North and South poles are geographical points only. To be sure that you are there, you must check your position with maps and compasses. The first explorers who walked across the snowy wastes to reach the North and South poles found nothing there to distinguish the Poles from the surrounding snow and ice.

What is pack ice?

In winter the Antarctic ocean freezes into a thin sheet of ice. In summer the ice sheet breaks into pieces called ice floes. Waves and winds pile up the floes into masses of pack ice. In the Antarctic winter, the pack ice can be as much as 900 miles wide around the coast.

Antarctic icebergs are generally lower and flatter than Arctic icebergs (inset). These huge slabs of ice break off the Antarctic ice sheet. Most of an iceberg floats beneath the surface of the water; only a fraction shows above.

How much of an iceberg is invisible?

Icebergs are massive chunks of ice that break off from the tips of glaciers or from the edges of ice sheets. The ice then floats away. Only about one-ninth of a tall iceberg shows above water. The rest is hidden below the surface.

How big was the biggest iceberg?

The biggest icebergs are the great, flat bergs that break away from the Antarctic ice sheet. Along the edge of the Ross Ice Shelf in the Antarctic the ice cracks with the rise and fall of the tide. Icebergs break loose and drift north into the Pacific Ocean. The largest iceberg ever seen, in 1956, was over 12,400 square miles (bigger than Belgium).

How much of the world is covered by ice?

Just over a tenth of the land surface of the Earth is covered by ice all year round. Almost 90 percent of the world's ice is in the Antarctic. The rest is mostly in the Arctic and in glaciers which are found on every continent.

How high are the tallest icebergs?

The tallest icebergs come from the Arctic. The tallest ever seen, in 1958, towered 550 feet above the water level—about 100 feet taller than the Great Pyramid in Egypt.

Where are the world's longest glaciers?

Eight of the Earth's ten longest glaciers are in the Antarctic. The longest glacier in the world is the Lambert Glacier in East Antarctica, which has a total length of 309 miles.

Does it snow all the time in the Antarctic?

Surprisingly, the Antarctic gets very little snow, especially on the vast interior plateau. Here it is very dry as well as extremely cold, and only about 2 inches of snow falls in a year. Near the coast, where it is less cold and the air is moister, there is more snow—averaging 24 inches a year.

Why is it difficult to build on permafrost?

Permafrost (frozen soil) covers the whole of the Antarctic. There are also large expanses of permafrost in the Arctic. Any heated building standing on permafrost warms the soil beneath it, melting the ice. It begins to sink into the deep mud that results. Only by insulating buildings, to keep heat from reaching the permafrost, can this be prevented.

Forests

What is a forest?

A forest is a large area of land thickly covered with trees. A smaller area of tree-covered land is a wood. Some forests have only a few species, or kinds, of trees in them. Others have many different species of trees packed together.

What were the first forests like?

The first forests developed in swamps about 365 million years ago, before there were any land animals. The plants in these prehistoric forests were not trees as we know them. They were club mosses, ferns, and horsetails. They grew as big as trees, and some were over 100 feet tall.

What happened to the giant horsetails?

Changes of climate over millions of years have shaped and reshaped the Earth's forests. By about 180 million years ago, the swamp forests had gone and in their place were forests of conifers, cycads, and ginkgos. The first flowering trees appeared about 130 million years ago.

How much of the Earth is covered with forest?

In prehistoric times, people had not begun to clear forests to make room for cities, farms, and factories. About 60 percent of the Earth's land area was forested then. Today only about 30 percent is covered by forest.

How many kinds of forest are there?

Different kinds of forest grow in different areas of the world. Climate determines which kind of forest grows. The six main kinds of forest are tropical rain forest, tropical seasonal forest (where the trees shed their leaves in the dry season), savanna, temperate deciduous forest (where the trees shed their leaves in winter), temperate evergreen forest, and boreal forest (taiga).

How did temperate forests appear?

About 65 million years ago, the Earth's climate turned cooler. This encouraged the spread of trees that thrive in temperate conditions (warm summers and cold winters). Temperate forests are common today in northern Europe and North America.

The world's vegetation zones. About 30 percent of the Earth is forest.

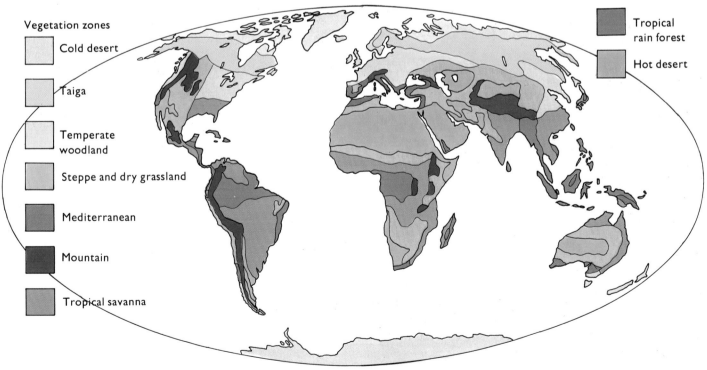

Vegetation zones
- Cold desert
- Taiga
- Temperate woodland
- Steppe and dry grassland
- Mediterranean
- Mountain
- Tropical savanna
- Tropical rain forest
- Hot desert

What is a taiga?

Taiga is another name for a boreal or northern forest. These forests grow in lands that have bitterly cold winters and short summers. The world's great boreal forests are in northern Europe, Asia, and North America. Most of the trees are evergreens such as spruce and pine.

Which forests have the most trees?

The richest forests on Earth are the tropical rain forests. In North America or Europe a small area of typical forest might contain about ten kinds of trees. The same area in a Brazilian or Indonesian rain forest might have over 100 different kinds of trees.

Why does a rain forest have so many different plants?

Tropical rain forests grow thickly because there is no cold winter or dry season to halt the growth of the trees and other plants. The sun shines almost every day, and even when it is cloudy the air remains warm and moist. Rain falls nearly every day. In such conditions the forest plants grow amazingly fast.

Do any plants grow on the rain forest floor?

Even in very dense rain forests, the lower layers get enough sunlight for some plants to grow. Waste, such as animal droppings and leaves, is broken down, releasing nutrients to feed the plants.

What trees grow in a deciduous forest?

Deciduous forests grow in regions with warm summers and cool winters. The trees in these forests have broad leaves. They include oak, beech, maple, and chestnut. These trees drop their leaves in autumn in order to reduce their water needs. Tree roots cannot absorb water very well from cold soil. A tree in full leaf needs more water than one which has stripped its branches ready for winter.

Where are there forests of gum trees?

Eucalyptus trees, called gum trees by Australians, make up most of Australia's forests and woodlands. There are many kinds, including the very tall blue gum (over 150 feet tall). Gum trees are unusual because they shed their bark every year. Gum trees are good for timber. Eucalyptus oil is made from the leaves and is used for treating colds.

How did the ice ages reduce the number of trees in northern Europe?

Before the ice ages, Europe and North America had the same dense forests, with many kinds of trees. When the ice sheet spread across northern Europe during the ice ages, many forest trees died out. They could not spread south to warmer regions and then "return" when the ice melted because high mountain ranges were in the way.

In the deciduous forests of temperate regions, different kinds of trees grow together. North American cool forests have a greater variety of trees than the forests of Europe.

Why do some tropical forest trees shed their leaves?

Many tropical trees grow in forests where there is a definite wet and dry season every year. The trees shed their leaves in the dry season to conserve water, and new growth quickly appears when the rains come.

Why did North America's forests survive the ice ages?

North America was affected by the ice ages like Europe, but its forests recovered better from the cold and ice. Forest trees migrated, spreading southward into warmer regions and returning when the ice had melted. Most North American mountains range from north to south so they were less of a barrier to the migrating trees. Today North America's cool forests have about ten times as many tree species as a similar European forest.

Where is the tree line?

Some trees such as the douglas fir grow high in the mountains. However, at some point on a high mountain the climate becomes too harsh for any trees to grow. The forest thins out, finally giving way to bare mountainside. The tree line is the highest point at which trees can grow.

The tropical rain forest is multi-storied, with the different layers supporting their own animal populations. Shrubs and creepers grow in the lower layers, provided the tree cover above is open enough to let sunlight reach them.

Where is the canopy in a rain forest?

The tops of the tallest trees in a rain forest make up the canopy. The canopy receives the most sunlight, and it grows thickly. It can form a dense roof, shadowing plants lower down. The tallest trees grow up through the lower layers, toward the sunlight. In the canopy live many animals such as monkeys, birds, and insects.

How do forests conserve water?

Forest soils soak up heavy rain, which filters through the earth to become groundwater, feeding streams, lakes, and wells. In this way forests prevent the rapid runoff of water after rain.

Conifers can grow in thin soils and tolerate cold better than deciduous trees.

What is the tundra?

The tundra is a zone near the Arctic where the climate is too cold and dry for trees. Most of the tundra is snow-covered much of the year. Mosses, lichens, and tough grasses are the only plants that can grow on the tundra.

Where are the steppes?

The steppes are dry, grassy plains. The central Asian steppes are the most widely known, but there are also steppes in North America. Steppes are found in regions with hot summers and cold winters. The grasses on the steppes are short and sparse. There are few trees.

How are prairies different from steppes?

Prairies are grasslands that receive more rainfall than steppes. Prairie grasses grow taller and thicker on rich, dark soil.

Where was the world's largest prairie?

The great prairie of the American Midwest once stretched from southern Texas north into Canada. It was the biggest on Earth, and in places the grass was as tall as a person. Today little remains of the original prairie. Since the 1800s, people have plowed it and planted it with crops such as wheat.

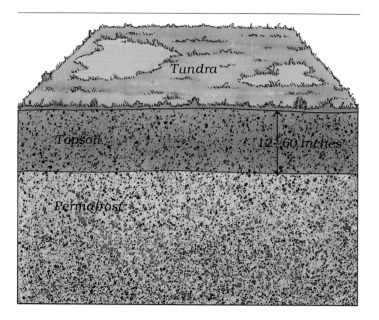

A cross section of the tundra shows a thin layer of topsoil and below, a frozen layer called the permafrost.

What is savanna?

Savanna is tropical grassland. It is found in hot regions with both rainy and dry seasons. On the African savanna, the rainy season lasts for only four months. The grassy plains there are dotted with acacia and baobab trees.

Why are grasslands so rich in animal life?

Grasslands provide a great deal of food for animals to eat. There are few trees, but the grasses and other plants provide homes for many insects, seed-eating birds, and rodents. Large grazers such as bison and antelope also live there, as well as the predators, such as wolves and lions, that feed on them.

How did grazing animals shape the grasslands of today?

Grazing animals are always nibbling away at vegetation. They can "prune" trees by eating all the branches up to a certain height. Giraffes, for example, cause many acacia trees to become mushroom-shaped by eating all the twigs as high as they can reach. Grazing actually encourages grasses to grow. As their older leaves are eaten, plants send out new side-shoots which soon produce new leaves.

Tundra vegetation is mostly stunted shrubs, herbs, mosses, and lichen. These cold-resistant plants provide food for grazing reindeer.

Where are the llanos and the pampas?

The llanos are the rolling grassy plains of South America. They are found mainly in Colombia and Venezuela. Farther south in Argentina are the huge grassy plains called the pampas. These temperate grasslands of South America are similar to the prairies of North America.

How do savannas survive a fire?

Savannas or tropical grasslands have a very hot dry season. Fires often sweep across savannas. Young trees are killed by the flames, but the grass usually survives because its roots escape scorching. Red oat grass, common on the African savanna, has seeds that work deep enough into the soil to escape being burned. When the rainy season comes, new grass springs up all over the savanna.

How is heathland created?

Some heathlands—a type of open shrubland—are natural. Strong salt-laden winds make such places along coasts inhospitable to trees, and only shrubs such as heather and bracken thrive. Heathlands elsewhere are sometimes created when people clear forests. The soil quickly loses its nutrients. Scrub vegetation takes over. Grazing by sheep and burning (to clear the land) prevents young trees from growing and keeps the heathland as heath.

Cattle ranching is one of the main farming activities on the grasslands.

Where are the world's main temperate grasslands?

The prairie of North America, the pampas and llanos of South America, and the steppes of eastern Europe and central Asia are the chief temperate grasslands.

A stretch of heathland. Natural vegetation on these uplands includes heather and bracken.

LIFE ON EARTH

How did life on Earth begin?

The Earth had existed for at least 3 billion years before the first signs of life appeared. As the fiery planet cooled, its atmosphere formed. Rains filled the seas, and in the seas life began. How it began is not known for sure. Maybe lightning provided the energy to start chemical reactions in the primeval "soup" of elements on the young planet. Perhaps minerals from the rocks formed and reformed new chemical combinations innumerable times. However it happened, an unusual chemical combination appeared: a living cell that could use energy to feed itself and reproduce copies of itself.

Life began as radiation and electrical storms energized chemicals to create the organic molecules that formed the first cells.

What was the Earth like when life began?

When life first appeared on Earth, the planet was very different from the world we know now. The land was bare, rocky, and mostly flat, for mountains and valleys had only just begun to form. Shallow seas covered most of the Earth, and it was in these seas that the first life forms appeared.

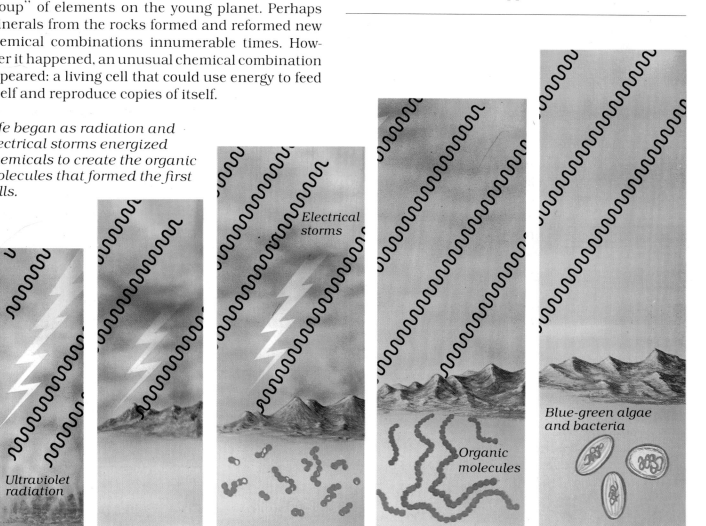

Electrical storms

Organic molecules

Blue-green algae and bacteria

Ultraviolet radiation

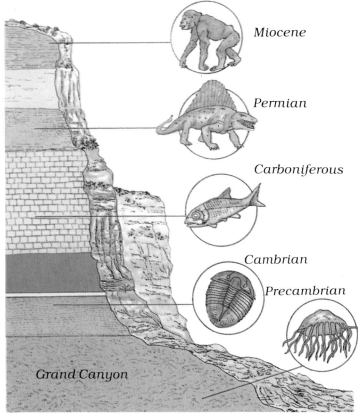

Miocene

Permian

Carboniferous

Cambrian

Precambrian

Grand Canyon

A cutaway of the Grand Canyon. Each layer of rock yields fossils recording the evolution of life.

What are fossils?

Fossils are found in rocks such as sandstone which was once soft sand or mud. Fossils are the marks or hardened remains of plants and animals that once lived on Earth. The most common fossils are the shells, teeth, or bones of animals or the tough outer skins of plants. Soft parts are not often preserved.

How do we discover fossils?

Fossils are found when ancient rocks are exposed. This may be by weathering from wind or rain or, sometimes, by quarrying or mining. Sometimes scientists can remove a whole dinosaur skeleton, bone by bone, from the rock.

How did living things change the Earth's atmosphere?

The first living things were more plantlike than animal-like. They could use the Sun's energy to change carbon dioxide gas and water into sugars (for food) and oxygen. The unwanted oxygen was freed into the atmosphere. Some oxygen changed to ozone, forming a thin layer around the Earth that absorbed harmful ultraviolet rays from the Sun. Gradually, the Earth changed into a planet able to support animals and plants.

How is a living thing unique?

Two things made the first living cell startlingly different from anything else yet on Earth. It drew energy from other chemicals in the seawater to feed itself, and it could reproduce, or make identical copies of itself.

How can geologists tell that one rock is older than another?

Over millions of years the chemicals in rocks change. Geologists measure how much the material in one rock has changed and compare this with other rocks. In this way they can tell how old different rocks are.

How is a fossil formed?

A fossil is the result of a death millions of years ago. Let us suppose a dinosaur dies beside a river or on the seashore. The soft body parts rot away while the hard parts, such as bones, are buried in mud. Over millions of years, layer upon layer of mud buries the bones deeper. The mud hardens into rock. Water seeping through the rock dissolves the bones. Minerals replace the bone material, forming exactly the same shape. A fossil skeleton of the dinosaur is preserved in the rocks.

How fossils are formed: an animal dies and its bones are buried in mud: the mud slowly hardens into rock and a fossil skeleton is preserved.

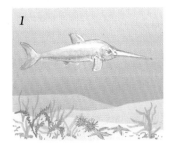

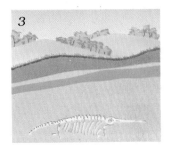

79

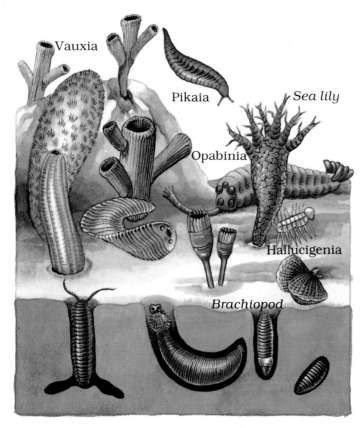

Life in the Cambrian seas. There were sponges (Vauxia), sea lilies, brachiopods, worms (Pikaia), and strange many-legged animals such as Hallucigenia and Opabinia.

Who were the first fossil-hunters?

About 2,500 years ago a Greek named Xenophanes was puzzled by the fossils he found. There were fish and seashells, yet they were a long way from the sea. The solution to this mystery was not uncovered until many years later. Leonardo da Vinci and others concluded that fossils were the remains of long-dead animals. Scientists realized that some areas of land had once been covered by the oceans, which explained Xenophanes' unusual finds.

How do we know about life in Cambrian times?

The animals that swam, crawled, and floated in Cambrian seas have been left behind as fossils. The most famous Cambrian "time capsule" is a rock formation in Canada called the Burgess Shale. It contains fossils of soft-bodied creatures as well as animals with shells.

What was life like in Cambrian times?

The period of time that geologists call the Cambrian period began about 570 million years ago. It lasted 70 million years. Cambrian animals lived in the sea. They had advanced from single-celled creatures to more advanced animals that swam and crawled. There were worms, jellyfish, snails, and starfish. Trilobites scuttled about on the sea floor.

When did fish first appear?

The early animals were invertebrates—animals with no backbones. They were either soft (jellyfish) or shelled (trilobites). The first animals with backbones (vertebrates) were fish. They appeared toward the end of the Cambrian period. The first fish had no jaws. They fed by sucking up bits of dead animals from the sea bottom.

When was the Age of Fishes?

About 410 million years ago, the Devonian period began. Many new kinds of fish swam in the seas, and this is why the Devonian period is known as the Age of Fishes. The newer fish had jaws and swam freely, chasing and eating other animals. All had a heavy armor of bony plates and scales. Among them were the ancestors of modern sharks and rays.

The first fish with bony skeletons appeared in the Devonian period. Most were lobe-finned (their fins had a lobe, or fleshy middle). These fins eventually evolved into legs, for walking.

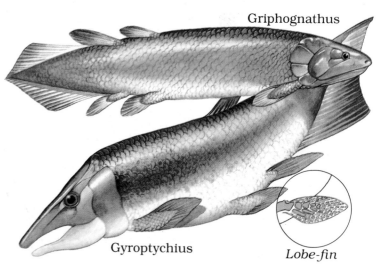

When did plants first grow on land?

About the same time as jawed fish appeared in the seas in the Devonian period, plants moved from the water to the land. They had to make two major adaptations: instead of floating in water, they had to support their own weight on a stiff stem; they also had to develop roots to anchor themselves in the soil and to take in food and water.

What were the first land animals?

The first creatures to move to the land were the ancestors of today's insects and spiders. They fed on the first land plants and on one another.

Why did some fish leave the water?

Fish that could breathe in air as well as in water were the first to move onto land. Here they found plenty of new food among the plants and insects but no rivals or predators.

Which modern animals give clues as to how the first animals moved onto the land?

There are fish alive today that can breathe air. The African lungfish is an example. It can survive inside a burrow in a dried-up riverbed. Another fish, the little mudskipper, uses its front fins as legs to crawl out of the water to find food. The first fish to crawl on land must have looked like a cross between these two.

What were the first amphibians like?

The first amphibians were animals that could live on land and in water. Among the earliest such creatures was the newtlike *Ichthyostega*. Measuring just under 3 feet long, it lived about 400 million years ago.

When did giant dragonflies hunt?

During the Carboniferous period, swampy forests flourished in the hot, damp climate. This was ideal for insects, spiders, millipedes, and other invertebrates. Through the undergrowth crawled millipedes that were 6 feet long, and in the air above, dragonflies that were as large as sea gulls hunted their insect prey.

Era	Period	Epoch	Millions of years ago
CENOZOIC	Quaternary	Recent	
			0.01
		Pleistocene	
			2
	Tertiary	Pliocene	
			5
		Miocene	
			25
		Oligocene	
			35
		Eocene	
			60
		Paleocene	
			65
MESOZOIC	Cretaceous		
			145
	Jurassic		
			210
	Triassic		
			245
PALEOZOIC	Permian		
			285
	Carboniferous		
			360
	Devonian		
			410
	Silurian		
			440
	Ordovician		
			505
	Cambrian		
			570
	Precambrian		

Geological time is measured in eras, periods, and epochs, stretching back millions of years.

How do geologists measure time?

In studying the Earth's history, we talk about stretches of time too long to imagine. Geologists have divided the Earth's history into periods. Each period lasted millions of years. Different plants and animals lived in different periods.

When was the Age of Ferns?

Ferns grew abundantly in the Carboniferous period (360 to 290 million years ago). There were vast, swampy forests with club mosses, horsetails, and many fernlike plants. Many fernlike fossils are found in coal, which was formed at this time.

Extinct Animals

Why were reptiles better suited for land life than amphibians?

The first amphibians, the ancestors of today's frogs and toads, were the first backboned animals on land. They could leave the water for some time, but had to return to it to lay their eggs. About 300 million years ago the first reptiles appeared. These animals looked like amphibians, but their eggs had tough shells and could be laid on land. This meant the reptiles could roam far from water.

Why did many of the early reptiles die out suddenly?

No one knows for certain why many of the reptiles disappeared. At the end of the Permian period (about 245 million years ago) more than half the animals and plants on Earth died out. Among them were many strange reptiles. There have been other mass extinctions from time to time in the Earth's history. This one may have been caused by changes in sea level and climate.

Were the big dinosaurs fierce hunters?

Some of the big dinosaurs were meat-eaters. But the largest of all were vegetarians. Some dinosaurs were the biggest land animals that have ever lived. *Brachiosaurus* was so tall it could have peered over the top of a 3-story building. *Diplodocus* stretched 100 feet from head to tail. There were even bigger animals, such as *Ultrasaurus* that probably weighed well over 100 tons. These enormous animals were peaceful and not very intelligent plant-eaters. They were plentiful in the Jurassic period when food for them was readily available in the lush, warm forests.

Stegosaurus

Stegosaurs were armored dinosaurs with spikes or plates along their backs.

When did dinosaurs rule the Earth?

For about 160 million years (from 225 million years ago to 65 million years ago) a group of reptiles called dinosaurs were the most successful animals on Earth. Some were small but others were giants.

Why are similar dinosaur remains found in places far apart?

When dinosaurs first appeared on Earth, the continents were still joined together. Animals could roam freely from what is now Africa to what is now North America. Fossils of the same kind of dinosaur have been found in East Africa and the United States. Since these animals lived and died, the continents have drifted apart, and with them the rocks containing the dinosaur fossils.

Eogyrinus

An early amphibian, Eogyrinus, meaning "early frog." It had a long, flat tail and probably spent much of its time in water, like a newt.

Why did some dinosaurs have armor?

Body armor is a useful defense for an animal. The armored dinosaur *Hylaeosaurus* had a thick covering of spikes and bony plates. *Triceratops* had horns and a massive bony shield to protect its head and neck. The 30-foot-long *Ankylosaurus* had a huge body covered in spikes and a clublike tail that it swung to beat off any attack.

Could dinosaurs live in the Arctic?

Yes, but the Arctic was not as cold as it is now. The Earth was much warmer during the Age of Dinosaurs, and the weather was similar all over the planet. Dinosaur bones have been found in rocks within the Arctic Circle, where it is now far too cold for reptiles to live.

How could such enormous animals survive?

The giant dinosaurs were much bigger than elephants, the largest land animals alive today. They needed huge amounts of food every day. The Earth was warm, and there was plenty of vegetation in the swamps and forests. Their huge size gave these lumbering giants protection against the meat-eating dinosaurs.

Mammoth

Pteranodon

Pteranodon *had batlike wings.*

When did reptiles fly?

Insects had taken to flying in the air long before reptiles joined them. The first flying reptiles simply glided from trees, using flaps of skin on their ribs as wings. The first reptiles that could fly by flapping their wings were the pterosaurs (about 200 million years ago). Some were no bigger than pigeons, but the biggest was the size of a small airplane. It measured 50 feet from one wing tip to the other.

Which were the most fearsome dinosaurs?

The most terrible of the meat-eating dinosaurs were creatures such as *Allosaurus*, which lived in Jurassic times (180–130 million years ago) and *Tyrannosaurus rex* of the Cretaceous period (130–65 million years ago). These animals were up to 40 feet long, and their jaws were lined with razor-sharp teeth. Some other hunting dinosaurs had huge, knifelike claws.

Which dinosaurs bellowed by breathing out hard?

Duck-billed dinosaurs had remarkable bony lumps or crests on their heads. Each group of these dinosaurs had a different shaped head. By making models of their skulls and blowing through the air passages, scientists think they have discovered the function of these odd head ornaments. They were trumpets. When the animal breathed out hard, the air rushed through the tubes in its bony head, making a bellowing noise, presumably to attract mates or warn of danger.

The woolly mammoth had long hair to protect it from the severe cold of the ice ages.

What happened to the dinosaurs?

There are no living dinosaurs today. All these amazing creatures seem to have died out at the end of the Cretaceous period (65 million years ago). Land dinosaurs, huge sea reptiles, and flying pterosaurs all vanished.

Why did the dinosaurs vanish?

The dinosaurs' disappearance remains a scientific puzzle. One answer may be that the Earth's climate grew cooler, and the warm forests dwindled; with the loss of their habitats, they died out. Another answer may lie in outer space. Had the Earth been hit by a comet or huge meteorite, there would have been an immense explosion. Dust rising into the atmosphere would have blotted out the Sun's warmth. The plants on which the dinosaurs fed would have died out, leading to the extinction of the dinosaurs.

Which animals replaced the dinosaurs?

The animals that survived when the dinosaurs died out were water creatures such as crocodiles, turtles, lizards (which could hibernate), and insects. There were also small furry animals—mammals—that were warm-blooded and intelligent and could thrive even in changeable conditions.

How big were turtles in prehistoric times?

Fossil turtles are generally like the turtles alive today. But some, such as *Archelon* ("ancient turtle") were huge, up to 13 feet long, and bigger than any modern sea turtle.

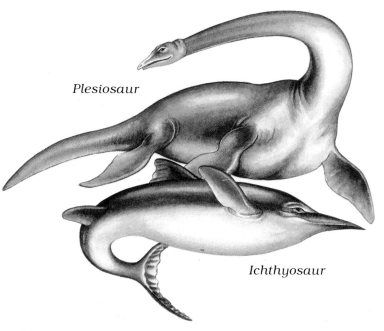

Plesiosaur

Ichthyosaur

Plesiosaurs had long necks and paddle-shaped flippers. Ichthyosaurs looked more like dolphins.

Which animals lived in the prehistoric oceans?

Fish, turtles, sharks, and crocodiles swam in the prehistoric oceans, as well as other, stranger creatures. They included plesiosaurs, which had long necks and paddle-like legs for swimming. Ichthyosaurs were like dolphins with long snouts, and mosasaurs were fierce animals with huge heads.

How did birds evolve?

Birds arose from small dinosaurs, but were not directly related to the flying pterosaurs. Prehistoric birds, such as *Archaeopteryx*, appeared during the Jurassic period. *Archaeopteryx* had wings with feathers but could not fly very far. On its wing tips were claws, probably used to cling to the branches of trees.

The ancestors of crocodiles, turtles, and lizards lived alongside the dinosaurs.

Turtle

Crocodile

Lizard

Earth's Animals

How many animals are alive today?

There are nearly 1.3 million species of animals on Earth today. About 96 percent are invertebrates (animals without backbones). There are almost certainly millions more species still unknown. Some experts think that there are up to 30 million more species of insects yet to be discovered.

Where do no animals live?

Animals live on land, in the ocean, and in the air. There is hardly a spot on Earth where some animals have not made their homes. However, there are no animals on the Moon.

Why did owls become silent flyers?

Owls are excellent night-hunters. They can see well in poor light, and the feathers on the edges of their wings are soft. This allows owls to swoop down silently on their prey—usually small mammals. They adapted to night-hunting in the course of their evolution. Owls with poor eyesight and noisy wings could not get much food. These poor hunters did not breed well and so died out.

When is a hedgehog not a hedgehog?

A hedgehog is not a hedgehog when it's a tenrec. Hedgehogs in Europe eat insects, snuffling through dead leaves to find them. On the island of Madagascar in the Indian Ocean there are no hedgehogs, but there is an animal called a tenrec. It looks and behaves like a hedgehog, with spines for protection against predators. This is an example of what scientists call *convergent evolution*—animals that have similar ways of life coming to look alike.

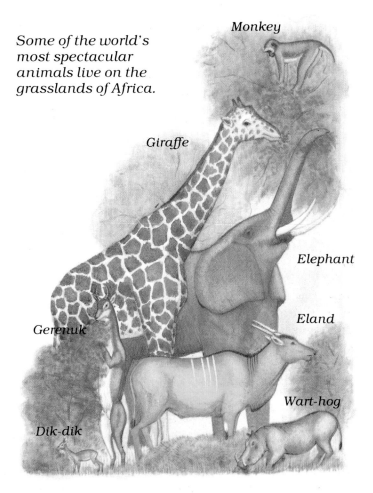

Some of the world's most spectacular animals live on the grasslands of Africa.

Monkey

Giraffe

Elephant

Eland

Gerenuk

Wart-hog

Dik-dik

How can animals adapt to living together?

Every plant and animal species has evolved its own way of life. Each occupies its own place in the natural habitat, called an ecological niche. Each animal or plant is adapted to its own niche. Very similar species can live side by side, with just a slight difference in their habits.

Are there more mammals than other vertebrates?

No. There are over 4,000 species of mammals. This puts mammals at the bottom of the vertebrate league table, along with amphibians. They are outnumbered by reptiles (over 6,500 species), birds (around 8,800 species) and fish (over 21,000 species).

The tenrec of Madagascar. The survival of many of Madagascar's unique animals is threatened as the forests they live in are destroyed.

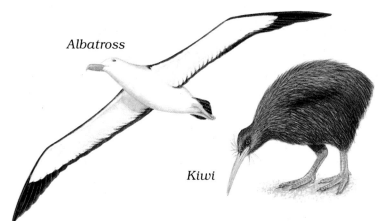

Albatross

Kiwi

An albatross, the most graceful of fliers, and the little flightless kiwi

Do all birds fly?

Birds are the animals best adapted to life in the air, but not all birds fly. The ostrich has wings but is too big and heavy to fly. Penguins have wings that have become flippers for swimming. The kiwi is a flightless New Zealand bird with tiny wings and no tail.

Why do birds sing?

Birds sing to attract other birds of the same species or to warn them off. Males sing to attract females as mates. The song also warns other males that the singer has its own territory and will defend it.

Can animals live without drinking?

Desert animals such as jerboas (small jumping rodents) live in places where water is extremely hard to find. The jerboa gets the water it needs from the plants it eats and does not need to drink. Camels can go for days without water, but when they reach an oasis they drink a lot—up to 53 gallons a day.

Which is the biggest animal on Earth?

Whales are the biggest animals on Earth. The largest is the blue whale, which is now rare because it has been hunted. It can be 100 feet long and weigh as much as 160 tons.

One blue whale can grow to be as heavy as 25 African elephants.

How do fish breathe in water?

Like most other animals, fish need oxygen to live. Land animals breathe in oxygen from the air. Fish take it from the water in which they live. A fish has special gills on either side of its head. To breathe, the fish swallows water and passes it through the gills, where oxygen is taken into the bloodstream.

What do bright colors often mean?

Many insects have brightly colored bodies or wings. These colors act as a warning to predators to keep away. The yellow and black stripes of a wasp, for instance, warn other animals to leave the wasp alone or risk being stung.

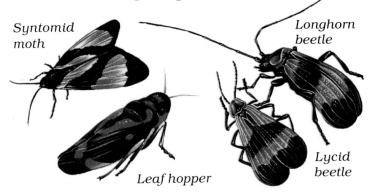

Syntomid moth

Longhorn beetle

Leaf hopper

Lycid beetle

Three of these four insects are "mimics." Only the orange-banded lycid beetle is poisonous. Color imitation is a good defense against birds.

Are there animals without eyes?

Eyes help an animal to see its food and to avoid being attacked by a predator. Sea anemones are water animals that simply wait for food to drift past. They taste unpleasant, so few animals eat them. Sea anemones therefore do not need eyes for protection. Cave animals and animals that live underground are also blind. Eyes are of no use to them, but senses of smell, hearing, and touch are.

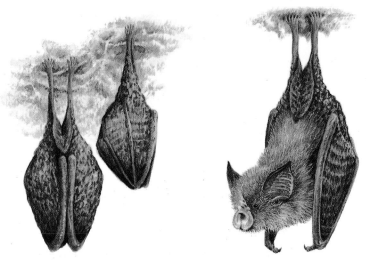

The lesser horseshoe bat

Which is the only flying mammal?

Some so-called flying animals simply glide. The only true flyers among mammals are the bats. Unlike birds, a bat has no feathers. Its wings are made of thin skin stretched over very long finger bones. Bats fly by flapping their wings, just as birds do.

Why do animals sleep through winter?

In cold countries some animals sleep through the winter. This winter sleep is called hibernation. The animals hibernate when there is little food or drinking water around or when the weather is very cold. While asleep the animals' bodies need very little energy to stay alive. The animals do not need to eat but live off fat stored during the summer.

Do bears hibernate?

Although female bears sleep most of the winter in snug dens, most scientists do not consider bears to be true hibernators. They give birth to their cubs during this time. On warm days they emerge to see if there is any food.

Why do emperor penguins keep their eggs on their feet?

Very few animals can live in the freezing cold of the Antarctic. The emperor penguin spends its whole life there. It is so cold that the birds cannot leave their eggs on the ice because the eggs would freeze. The penguin therefore carries its egg on its feet under a fold of warm skin.

What is unusual about many Australian animals?

Australia is the main home of marsupials (animals that carry their young in pouches) such as kangaroos, wallabies, wombats, and koalas. Australia is separated from other continents by large expanses of ocean and has been isolated for millions of years. Its marsupial animals have evolved on their own, safe from competition from more advanced animals elsewhere.

The kangaroo is one of Australia's distinctive marsupials. The female carries her baby in a pouch on her body until it is big enough to look after itself.

Which sea creatures can climb trees?

Crabs have eight walking legs and an extra pair armed with pincers for grabbing and holding prey. Whether on the seabed or on dry land, almost all crabs walk by scuttling sideways. Some even climb trees.

What happened when rabbits went to Australia?

In Europe, rabbits have many natural predators such as foxes, weasels, and eagles. These keep the numbers of rabbits down. Settlers from Europe took rabbits to Australia in the 1800s. The rabbits ran wild, bred rapidly, and soon became pests. The rabbit had no natural enemies because it was not a native Australian animal. The rabbits became such pests that farmers had to put up rabbit-proof fences to protect their crops.

Why must reptiles live in warm climates?

Reptiles are cold-blooded. This means they can go for long periods without eating, because a cold-blooded animal needs less energy to stay alive. Reptiles are active in warm temperatures. When it gets cold, their body temperatures drop and they become sluggish. Reptiles are therefore found in warm climates, where the plants and insects they eat are also available all year round.

Reptiles are active in the Sun's warmth. They become sluggish as the temperature falls.

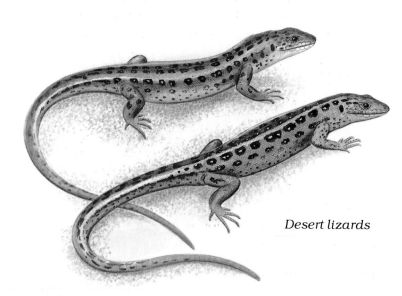

Desert lizards

The Japanese spider crab is up to 12 inches across its body, with legs up to 10 feet long.

Can animals freeze solid?

A salamander froze in ice when hibernating and remained in deep freeze for 90 years. It was warmed up and restored to life by Russian scientists. Antarctic fish have an "antifreeze" chemical in their bodies. The chemical stops the water in the animals' bodies from turning to ice when they are swimming in subzero temperatures. Polar mammals such as seals and polar bears keep themselves warm by burning up food energy.

Why do some animals change color in winter?

When winter snows come, some animals change color. Their winter coats are white to camouflage them against the snow. Animals that change color include the ermine, Arctic hare, Arctic fox, and ptarmigan. When the snow melts again in springtime, they molt their white coat and return to their usual color.

How can you tell one Galapagos tortoise from another?

The Galapagos Islands are in the Pacific Ocean, west of South America. They are home to giant tortoises. All the tortoises on the islands belong to the same species. Yet the tortoises on different islands look slightly different. They have slightly different shells or longer necks. These changes are related to the kind of foods available on each of the different islands and are a good example of evolution in progress.

Which insects have royal families?

Social insects live together in groups called colonies. They build large nests. Bees, ants, and termites are social insects. Each colony has a queen, and only she lays eggs. All the members of the colony are the queen's children. Most grow up to be workers. Some are soldiers, and a few are males that mate with new queens.

Why do mountain insects crawl rather than take to the air?

Mountaintops are not suitable for flying insects because the strong winds are likely to blow them away. Not surprisingly, therefore, mountain insects crawl, keeping a grip on the ground.

Can insects live in the sea?

Only one insect lives near seawater. The marine springtail lives on the surface of the water, usually in small beach pools. On its body are fine hairs which trap a layer of air. If the springtail is washed out to sea by a wave, it can live for up to five days on this emergency air supply.

Which animals light up the darkness?

Deep-sea fish live in a cold, dark world. There is no sunlight. In order to attract mates and to lure prey, some deep-sea fish have developed their own lights. The light is made chemically by organs called *photophores*.

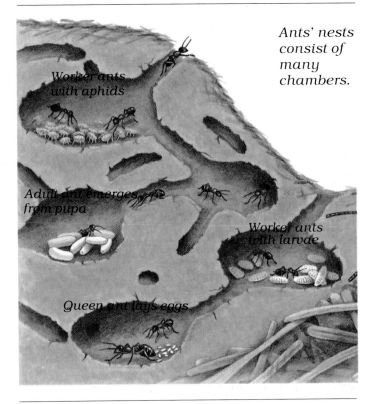

Ants' nests consist of many chambers.

Worker ants with aphids

Adult ant emerges from pupa

Worker ants with larvae

Queen ant lays eggs

Which monkeys hang by their tails?

Many New World or American monkeys have prehensile or grasping tails. The monkeys of Africa and Asia have tails just as long, but they lack this extra ability.

Which mammals drink seawater?

Dolphins can drink seawater. A dolphin's kidneys can remove the salts from the water it drinks. The salts are concentrated in urine and passed out of the body as waste. No human could drink seawater without getting ill and probably dying.

Are polar bears really white?

Polar bears have white fur to help them blend in with the Arctic snow and so avoid being spotted by the animals they hunt for food. Actually polar bear fur is transparent. It looks white because the hollow see-through fur reflects sunlight. The long hairs are thick and oily and help to keep the bear warm in the icy conditions.

The polar bear's dense coat helps protect it from the bitter Arctic cold.

Plants

What are the simplest plants like?

The first plants appeared about 3 billion years ago. They were single-celled algae and diatoms. Such plants are very tiny. A single drop of water can contain 500 diatoms.

Which are the most successful plants?

The flowering plants make up the biggest and most successful plant group. There are more than 250,000 different kinds. They include grasses, cacti, trees, peas and beans, vines, potatoes, spices, and many garden and wild flowers. All these plants generate flowers. They are the most advanced members of the plant kingdom.

Which is the oldest plant?

Plants live much longer than animals. The world's oldest tree is the bristlecone pine. One bristlecone in Arizona sprouted over 4,600 years ago—at the time the Great Pyramid of Egypt was being built. Yet it is not the oldest plant. The creosote plant of California and some Antarctic lichens may well be 10,000 years old.

The bristlecone pine of North America

Can plants live without sunlight?

All green plants need sunlight because they use the Sun's energy to make their food. The food-making process, called photosynthesis, takes place mainly in the leaves using a substance called chlorophyll. A green plant kept in darkness withers and dies. Mushrooms, which feed on plants or dead matter, can live in darkness.

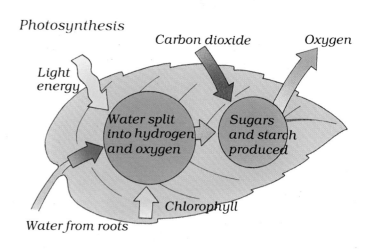

Photosynthesis

Carbon dioxide

Oxygen

Light energy

Water split into hydrogen and oxygen

Sugars and starch produced

Chlorophyll

Water from roots

How do plants make their food?

Only plants can make their own food. Green plants use the energy from sunlight to turn water (from the soil) and carbon dioxide (from the air) into glucose (sugar). The plants use the glucose as food. They give off oxygen, which is left over from their food-making. Without this oxygen, no animals could live on the Earth.

Why do most plants have flowers?

Flowers help plants to reproduce themselves. The flower produces male and female cells (pollen and egg cells). It provides a way for the eggs to be fertilized by pollen from another plant. The flower also protects the egg cells as they grow into seeds and makes sure the seeds are spread so that a new generation of plants can grow.

How deep can a plant's roots go?

The plant with the longest roots is thought to be a wild fig tree in South Africa. A specimen of this plant was found which had roots nearly 400 feet underground.

Why do some plants have no flowers?

Mosses and ferns have no flowers because they do not produce seeds. Instead they reproduce by means of spores. The spores of ferns form on the leaves. The spore falls to the ground and develops into a heart-shaped structure called a *prothallus*. This produces male and female cells.

Which fruits explode?

A plant needs to spread its seeds to give each one the best possible chance of growing into a new plant. One way to spread seeds is to shoot them out from an exploding capsule or pod. Laburnum trees and other plants of the pea family have seeds in pods. When a laburnum pod dries out it splits. The two halves twist, flinging out the seeds.

Why do some plants have wings and parachutes?

The wind can spread a plant's seeds over long distances. Some seeds are light enough to blow about easily. Dandelions and thistles have fruits crowned with hairy plumes that act like parachutes. The seeds drift away on the wind. The fruit of some trees such as the birch, maple, and ash have wings. These spin like the blades of a helicopter as they carry the seed away.

The seeds and seedpods of many plants are specially designed to allow the wind to carry them away.

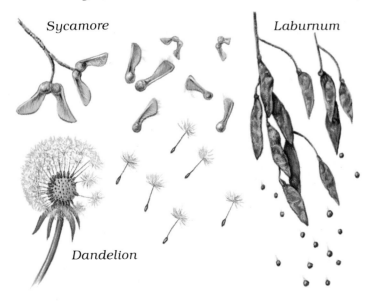

Sycamore

Laburnum

Dandelion

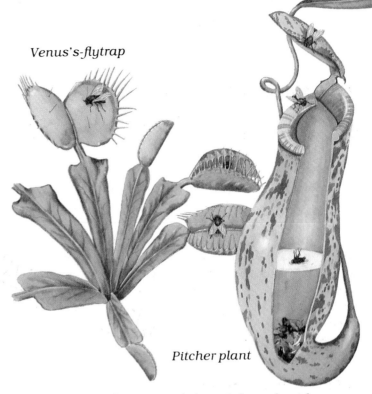

Venus's-flytrap

Pitcher plant

The Venus's-flytrap and the pitcher plant have developed sophisticated traps for their unsuspecting insect prey.

Can plants eat insects?

Insect-eating plants, like the sundew and Venus's-flytrap, live in poor, often boggy soil. The soil has few minerals to feed the plants. The plants have therefore developed traps to catch insects as an extra food source. The sundew's leaves are covered in sticky-tipped tentacles. The Venus's-flytrap catches insects in traps on the end of its leaves. Each trap snaps shut when an insect touches one of its trigger hairs. The insect is crushed and the plant breaks down its body with acid to obtain the food chemicals it needs.

Why do plant stems grow up and roots grow down?

Plants are affected by the Earth's gravity. They sense which is "up" and which is "down." No matter which way you plant a bean seed, the root always grows downward. The stem grows upward, seeking the light. The way plants react to gravity is controlled by hormones. If the plant begins to grow the wrong way, the hormones make it change direction.

How rare can a plant become?

Plants can become very specialized, living only in one small area. For example, there is only one Cafe marron tree in the world. It grows on Rodriguez Island in the Indian Ocean. Scientists have taken cuttings of the tree to propagate it (make new trees).

How high up can plants grow?

Many kinds of mosses, shrubs, and wild flowers can live on high mountains amid the cold, wind and snow. Most grow close to the ground, clinging to the rocks and thin soil. Flowering plants have been found growing over 20,000 feet up in the Himalaya Mountains of Asia.

What are the biggest living things on Earth?

The biggest living things on Earth are giant sequoia trees. These giant plants grow in California. The biggest sequoia is 274 feet tall and measures almost 115 feet around its trunk. It is thought to be 4,000 years old.

Which plant has the biggest flowers?

The largest flowers belong to the *Rafflesia*, or stinking corpse lily, of Southeast Asia. They measure 3 feet across. This flower smells like rotting meat, which is unpleasant to people but attractive to lots of insects that visit the flower and pollinate the plant.

Rafflesia

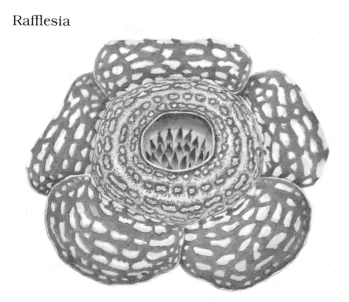

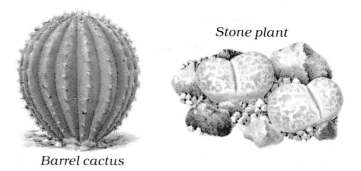

Stone plant

Barrel cactus

Desert plants, such as cacti, have evolved ways to lock up as much moisture as possible in their stems and leaves.

Why do plants need water?

Over 90 percent of a plant is water. Without water a plant cannot make food by photosynthesis. Water helps to keep the plant's cells rigid. If there is not enough water, the cells become limp, and the plant wilts. Most plants need a constant supply of water from their roots.

How do plants survive in the desert?

Desert plants such as cacti can live for months or even years without water. They have evolved ways of storing moisture in thick stems or swollen, fleshy leaves. Other desert plants store water in their roots. A desert plant may remain dried up and appear dead for years. When rain eventually falls, the desert blooms. The plants spurt into growth, making use of all the suddenly available moisture. Plants flower, pollinate, make seeds, and spread them in the space of only a few weeks.

Why do desert plants spread out?

Desert plants do not grow close together. If they did they would compete for the scarce food and water. Instead they spread out. Desert plants usually have long roots that spread out to catch as much moisture as possible.

Which plant has the longest leaves?

In Madagascar there is a palm tree called the raffia palm. Its leaves grow more than 40 feet long, and there have been trees with leaves 65 feet long and over 6 feet across. Slightly smaller are the fan-shaped leaves of the talipot palm.

Are all cacti small?

Most desert plants are economical with their growth: they are short or medium-sized. The exception is the giant saguaro cactus of the American Southwest. This tall, branching cactus can grow to a height of 50 feet or more. The saguaro has grooves and ridges along its trunk and branches. These swell or shrink depending on the amount of water the plant has stored inside.

Can a plant reproduce itself without making seeds?

Plants do not need to make seeds. They can split into two, they can grow buds that develop into new cells, they can make spores (as ferns do), or they can reproduce by vegetative propagation. This happens in strawberry plants. The plant sends out a long stem, called a runner, which sprouts roots. If the runner is then cut, its rooted part will grow into a new plant. Similarly, if you cut the eye, or bud, from a potato and plant it, it will make a new potato plant.

Why are some plants parasites?

Some plants, such as ivy or tropical lianas, use other plants as supports. This avoids spending energy on making their own stem stiff. However, they make their own food. Mistletoe is a part-parasite. It takes some food from the tree it clings to by piercing the bark with rootlike tubes, but it also has green leaves to make some food on its own. Other parasites take all their food from the "host" plant and make none of their own.

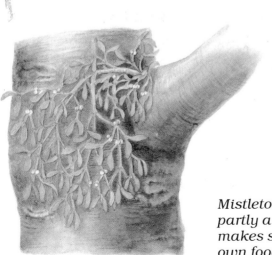

Mistletoe is only partly a parasite. It makes some of its own food.

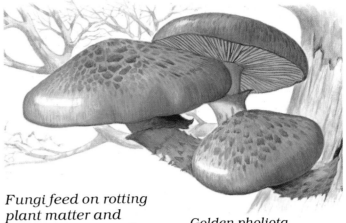

Fungi feed on rotting plant matter and can feed on the cells of other plants.

Golden pholiota mushroom

Which plants are not really plants?

Fungi are no longer classified as plants because they contain no chlorophyll and cannot make their own food, as green plants do. Instead they take food from other plants or scavenge on dead material such as old wood. Fungi produce chemicals that attack cellulose—the material of which green plant cells are made. In this way a fungus can feed on the cells of plants.

Why does wet paper go moldy?

Fungi grow on anything made of cellulose—food, clothes, wooden furniture, old books. Anyplace that is damp is a suitable home for the spores of molds and mildews, which are kinds of fungus.

How does gravity affect plants?

Plants are affected in various ways by their environment. Even if a seed or bulb is planted upside down, its roots will curl downward, toward the source of gravity. Its shoots grow up, toward the sunlight.

How do plants keep cool?

Plants lose water through tiny pores, or stomata, under their leaves. This loss is called transpiration. At the same time, the plant draws up water from the soil into its roots. The water lost through the leaves helps keep the plant cool. The flow of water up the stem from the roots brings with it vital minerals from the soil.

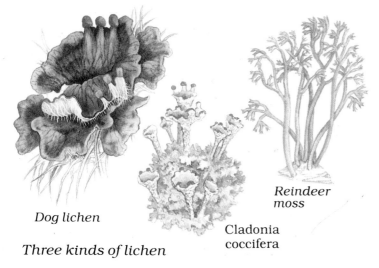

Dog lichen

Reindeer moss

Cladonia coccifera

Three kinds of lichen

Which plants have no roots, leaves, or flowers?

Lichens are simple plants with no roots, leaves, or flowers. They are actually a combination of an alga and a fungus living closely together. Some grow as crusty patches on rocks, trees, and walls. Lichens grow very slowly and to a very great age (10,000 years old). They are among the oldest known living things and can survive in places that are too bare, dry, cold, or hot for other plants.

How do seaweeds survive the pounding of the waves?

Seaweeds are tough plants. They are pounded by waves, and those on the shoreline are repeatedly soaked and dried out as the tides rise and fall. Many shore seaweeds have a branching foot which produces an adhesive to glue the plant to a rock. A jellylike coating helps to keep the plants from drying out. Many seaweeds have air-filled bladders to keep them afloat on the sunlit surface waters.

How many kinds of seaweed are there?

There are 7,000 kinds of seaweed, most of which grow near the shore where they can cling on to the rocks or seabed by the footlike "holdfast." Attached to the holdfast is a frond, which sways in the water. Most brown seaweeds live in cool seas, and some grow very large. Red seaweeds are commonest in warm seas. Green and blue-green seaweeds are found in warm and cold seas, but warm seas have the greatest variety.

Seaweeds grow completely under water or in the midtide zone. Above the high-tide mark, land plants begin to appear.

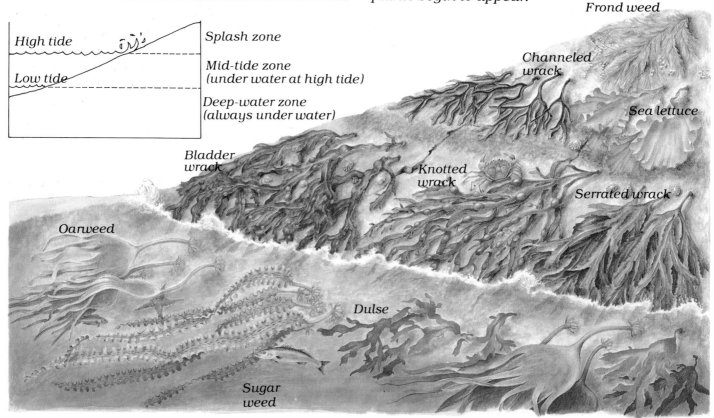

High tide — Splash zone

Low tide — Mid-tide zone (under water at high tide)

Deep-water zone (always under water)

Frond weed

Channeled wrack

Sea lettuce

Bladder wrack

Knotted wrack

Serrated wrack

Oarweed

Dulse

Sugar weed

Palm trees grow mainly in the tropics, but a few species are found in temperate climates.

Which trees have no branches?

Palm trees are unlike most other trees. They do not grow side branches and so do not grow thicker. They just get taller. The scars in the trunk of a palm tree are where leaves once grew. New leaves sprout from the top of the trunk. If this top is cut off, the palm tree dies.

Why do trees have bark?

The bark of a tree protects the living wood inside. It keeps moisture in and insects and parasites out. It also helps to protect the tree in very hot or very cold weather. Bark has two layers. The inside layer is a soft, living material rather like cork. The outer layer is a tough, dead shell.

What are the two main kinds of trees?

Conifers, such as spruce, pine, and fir, have needlelike leaves. They produce seeds in cones, not flowers. Most conifers are evergreen. They grow best in cooler climates. The other kind of tree is the broad-leaved flowering tree. Many are deciduous, shedding their leaves in the autumn. Others, such as holly, are evergreen. Many tropical trees are evergreen too. Others shed their leaves in the dry season and grow new leaves when the rains fall.

How do trees act as the Earth's "lungs"?

Trees play a vital part in keeping the Earth's atmosphere fit for animals and people to breathe. Trees take in carbon dioxide from the air and give off oxygen.

Why do conifers keep their leaves in winter?

Deciduous trees shed their leaves to avoid water loss and frost damage. Conifers keep their leaves. They do best in areas where water is scarce. Their leaves are so thin that they lose very little water.

Brittle tip

Acid reservoir

When touched, the tip of the hair on a nettle leaf pierces the skin and breaks off. Acid is injected, causing a nasty sting.

Stinging nettle

Why do nettles sting?

Most plants have defense systems, to keep animals from eating them. Thorns and spines are effective. The stinging nettle has hollow stinging hairs, which are activated by something touching the plant.

Do plants have clocks?

Many plants know what time of year it is with amazing accuracy. Some flowering plants bloom at exactly the same time every year. Like many animals, plants prepare for winter by storing food in their underground stems and roots. Their "clock" is controlled by the length of day and night, which changes steadily all year round.

PEOPLE AND PLACES

Africa

How big is Africa?

North America would fit comfortably into Africa with an area the size of Europe to spare! Africa has a land area of nearly 12 million square miles. It is more than 5,000 miles long from north to south and almost 5,000 miles wide from east to west.

Africa is mostly a huge jungle: true or false?

False. Most of Africa is either desert (40 percent) or grassy savanna (40 percent). Forests cover less than a fifth of Africa. Most of this African forest is rain forest.

Where are the Mountains of the Moon?

On the border between Uganda and Zaire in central Africa are the Ruwenzori Mountains. These snow-capped peaks are over 16,000 feet high. They were named the Mountains of the Moon by the early geographer Ptolemy, who in A.D. 150 drew a map showing the river Nile beginning its journey in these mountains.

What is the Great Rift Valley?

The Great Rift Valley is one of Africa's outstanding natural features: a series of valleys that cuts through eastern Africa. In some areas the rift in the Earth is over 1 mile deep and 60 miles wide. The Great Rift Valley is the result of volcanic movement. In certain places the rift has filled with water, creating some of Africa's greatest lakes (Mobutu Sese Seko, Edward, Nyasa, and Tanganyika) as well as the Red Sea.

How high is the land in Africa?

Compared to Asia or North America, Africa is relatively flat. The north, west, and center of the continent are mostly below 2,000 feet. Most of northern Africa is the huge plateau of the Sahara. The highest land in Africa is in the east and south. This region includes the Great Rift Valley and the grassy plains of the Eastern Highlands.

Until this century there were no big cities in Africa south of the Sahara Desert. Today modern cities grow ever larger. Thirty percent of Africa's people now live in towns and cities with tall buildings, and busy streets filled with vehicles can be found in many African countries.

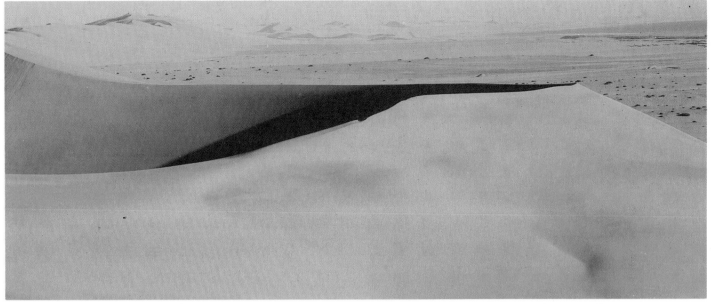

Is there much desert in Africa?

About 40 percent of Africa is desert. The Sahara Desert is enormous, covering much of the northern third of the continent. Other deserts are the Namib and the Kalahari in the southwest.

Which are Africa's greatest rivers?

Africa's biggest rivers are the Nile (the longest river in the world), followed by the Zaire (Congo), the Niger, and the Zambezi.

Where is the Tugela Falls?

The Tugela Falls is a series of five waterfalls on the Tugela River in South Africa. The highest fall is 1,350 feet high, and in all, the five falls drop 3,125 feet. This makes Tugela the second highest waterfall in the world.

Is there any snow in Africa?

Africa's highest mountain is in Tanzania in eastern Africa. It is Kilimanjaro or Uhuru ("freedom") and is 19,340 feet high. Kilimanjaro is an extinct volcano. Although very near the equator, the summit is always covered with snow.

Which is Africa's largest island?

The island of Madagascar, off the eastern coast of Africa, covers 227,000 square miles. It is the fourth biggest island in the world.

The Namib Desert in southwest Africa

When did people first live in Africa?

Africa was where human beings first evolved. Scientists have found bones and other remains of humanlike creatures that are older than any remains found elsewhere. These creatures lived more than 4 million years ago. About 2 million years ago the first true humans were living in Africa, hunting animals and gathering plants for food, and making the first stone tools.

Black Africans make up about 70 percent of Africa's population.

Victoria Falls

What is the "smoke that thunders"?

Near the Zambia-Zimbabwe border the Zambezi River plunges over Victoria Falls. This is Africa's most spectacular waterfall, 343 feet high and a mile wide. As the river pours over the falls, a great mist of spray rises into the air, and the thunder of the water can be heard far away. The African name for the falls is Mosi oa Tunya, which means "the smoke that thunders."

Why is drought a problem in Africa?

Rainfall in Africa is very uneven. Some parts of the continent, such as the western rain forests, get rain all year round. Drier areas may go for years without a shower. Much of Africa has one or two wet seasons each year. If these rains fail, crops do not grow and people starve. Drought (lack of rain) has been a cause of famine in the lands fringing the Sahara Desert and in Ethiopia in northeast Africa.

What is the harmattan?

The harmattan is an African wind. It blows from the Sahara Desert westward and southwestward from December to February. The harmattan is dry and also cool, because the desert is cooler at this time of year. It carries dust from the Sahara across neighboring countries.

Why is Africa a warm continent?

The equator runs across the middle of Africa, and all but a tenth of Africa is within the tropics. Temperatures are high all year round, and there is little difference between summer and winter. The Sahara Desert in the north is one of the hottest places in the world.

Which is Africa's largest country?

The biggest country in Africa is the Sudan. It has an area of over 900,000 square miles. The north is bleak desert, but in the south are grassy plains. The Nile River creates a huge marshy area, known as the sudd.

Most of the continent of Africa lies within the tropics.

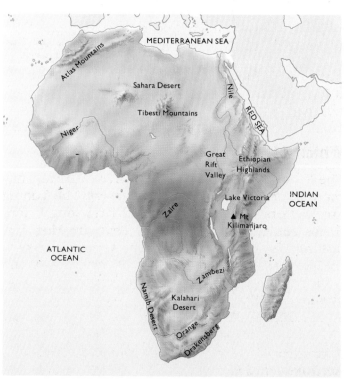

Giraffe

Eland

Zebra

Ostrich

Female impala

Impala

Guinea fowl

Animals found on the African savanna

How do the San survive in the desert?

The San are people of southwest Africa. A few still roam the Kalahari Desert, where there is little water and few trees. The San are skillful hunters and trackers, and they gather foods such as insects, roots, and berries. They can find drinking water underground in roots and wet sand. They can live in a land so harsh that outsiders would soon die of thirst and hunger. Like many Africans, the San are now giving up their traditional ways.

Which African men wear veils?

The Tuareg are nomads of northern Africa. They roam in or around the Sahara Desert. The Tuareg are Berbers, a people who lived here long before Arabs settled northern Africa. They are Muslims, but it is the Tuareg men, not the women, who hide their faces behind veils. Once the Tuareg raided and traded across the Sahara, but most have now abandoned their old desert life.

Nomads with their goats and camels in Eritrea, northeast Africa

How do Africa's nomads live?

Some Africans, such as the nomads of the Sahara region and northeast Africa, still follow traditional ways of life. These people wander with herds of camels, sheep, and goats. They have no settled homes but keep moving in search of fresh pasture for their animals.

Asia

Asia is the biggest continent and has the longest coastline.

How big is Asia?

Asia is the biggest continent. Its area of 17 million square miles is greater than North and South America put together and four times greater than Europe. The coastline of Asia is almost 80,000 miles long—more than three times the distance around the world at the equator.

Where are Asia's high and low points?

Asia has the highest and lowest points on the Earth. Mount Everest (over 29,000 feet above sea level) is the highest point. The shores of the Dead Sea (1,310 feet below sea level) are the lowest point.

Where are Asia's deepest gorges?

The deepest gorges cut by rivers are those made by the rivers Indus, Brahmaputra, and Ganges which flow through India and Pakistan. In places they are more than 3 miles deep.

Does Asia have more people than any other continent?

Yes. As well as covering one-third of the Earth's land surface, Asia has about three-fifths of the world's population. More than 3 billion people live in Asia.

Parts of Japan rank among the most densely populated areas of the world.

Which country has the most languages?

India has 14 major languages and more than 160 others. There are also 700 dialects (local or regional variations). Hindi is the official language of India, and many Indians also use English.

Which is Asia's highest waterfall?

The highest waterfall in Asia is called Jog or Garsoppa. It is in India on the Sharavati River and is 890 feet high.

Where is the Khyber Pass?

The Khyber Pass is in northwest Pakistan. Here the land is rugged and hilly. The pass is a route through the mountains to Afghanistan.

What is the Tonlé Sap?

The Tonlé Sap is a large lake in Cambodia, in Southeast Asia. Its waters cover some 4,000 square miles. The lake is formed by water from the Mekong River, the longest river in Southeast Asia (2,700 miles) and the fifth longest in Asia.

Hindus in India come to bathe in the holy Ganges River. India is the second most populous country in the world.

Which is the highest mountain in India?

To the north of India rise the mighty Himalayas, the highest mountains in the world. The highest peaks, including Mount Everest, are in Nepal, but India too has some towering peaks. The highest mountain in India is Nanda Devi in the western Himalayas, which is 25,647 feet high.

Where is the Roof of the World?

The Roof of the World is the name given to a region north of India where several mighty mountain ranges meet. Here are the highest mountains on Earth, including the peaks of the Himalayas, the Tien Shan, the Kunlun, the Karakoram, and the Pamirs.

In which country do people live longest?

Every country has a few people who live to an exceptionally great age—100 or more. In Japan the average life expectancy (the number of years a newborn baby can expect to live) is 77. This is even higher than in Europe or the United States. In some poor countries of Africa, the life expectancy is only 45–50.

How many islands make up Japan?

Japan is a bow-shaped chain of islands that stretches for about 1,100 miles. There are four main islands, called Honshu (the biggest), Hokkaido, Shikoku, and Kyushu. There are about 3,000 smaller islands.

Which is Japan's most famous mountain?

Japan has more than 160 volcanoes, about a third of which are active. The most famous is Fujiyama, or Mount Fuji. It is the highest mountain in Japan (12,388 feet). This cone-shaped volcano last erupted in 1707. To the people of Japan, Fujiyama is a sacred mountain.

Japan is a country of contrasts, between city and countryside and between old and new. Fujiyama is the highest peak in Japan and a sacred symbol to the people.

What are the Maldives?

The Maldives is a chain of low-lying coral islands in the Indian Ocean. Some of the islands belong to India. The rest make up the republic of the Maldives, a separate country. There are more than 2,000 islands, but fewer than 200 are big enough for people to live on.

Where is Angkor Wat?

Angkor Wat is a temple in Cambodia and the biggest religious building in the world. It was built by the Khmer people of Southeast Asia in the 1100s in honor of a Hindu god. Later, Buddhists added to the temple buildings. Angkor Wat was abandoned by the 1500s. Wooden buildings rotted away, and the stone temple was overgrown by forest. In the 1860s a Frenchman discovered the ruins.

A reconstruction of the magnificent temple of Angkor Wat in Cambodia. The temple covers an area of 1,200 square yards or one-fourth of an acre.

A town in Siberia, the "Wild East" of Russia

Where is Siberia?

East of the Ural Mountains lies Siberia, a wilderness of 4.9 million square miles stretching to the Pacific Ocean. Siberia is a region of vast forests, rivers, and frozen plains. Here are the coldest inhabited places in the world, where winter temperatures drop to −89°F.

Which is Asia's longest river?

The Chang Jiang, or Yangtze Kiang, in China is the longest river in Asia. It flows 3,915 miles into the South China Sea.

Which Asian city is sacred to three religions?

Jerusalem is a holy city for people of three faiths: Jews, Christians, and Muslims. Jerusalem was divided between Israel and Jordan until 1967; since then Israel has held all of the city. For Jews, Jerusalem is the ancient Hebrew capital, where King Solomon built the Temple. For Christians, the city is where Jesus Christ preached and was crucified. Muslims believe that the Prophet Muhammad rose to heaven from a rock in Jerusalem. The Dome of the Rock shrine now stands on the spot.

Which rivers are known as the "cradle of civilization"?

Ancient civilizations grew up near rivers. Rivers were trade routes and provided water for farming. Several great civilizations arose in Asia. The rivers Tigris and Euphrates in Mesopotamia (now Iraq) gave rise to the civilizations of Sumer and Babylon over 5,000 years ago. The Indus River valley in Pakistan was the center of another great ancient civilization, the Indus Valley civilization.

Where is Asia's biggest island?

The island of Borneo is the biggest island in Asia. Its 285,000 square miles are shared by three countries: Malaysia, Indonesia, and Brunei. Borneo is a mountainous island, and much of it is covered with dense rain forest, although logging companies are steadily cutting down the trees.

Where are the world's richest countries?

A country's wealth is measured in different ways. One way is to work out the average wealth per person (supposing that all the country's wealth could be divided equally between all its people). The oil-producing countries of the Middle East, such as the United Arab Emirates, then lead the way. They have small populations but enormous national wealth from selling oil.

Which is the only city situated on two continents?

Istanbul in Turkey lies in Europe and Asia. It is built on both banks of the Bosporus, the strait that separates these two continents, and is sometimes called the "Gateway to Asia." This great city has had three names. Founded by the ancient Greeks, it was first called Byzantium but was renamed Constantinople by the Romans in A.D. 330. In 1453 the Turks captured the city, and it became known as Istanbul.

Istanbul is a city with a great history. Santa Sophia (above), built as a church in A.D. 532, was later converted into a mosque by the Turks. It is now a museum.

Why is Bahrain a true desert island?

The small island of Bahrain in the Persian Gulf has hardly any rainfall. For several months of the year no clouds are seen and the total average annual rainfall is less than 4 inches. Despite being mostly desert, Bahrain is rich because it sells petroleum abroad.

Europe

Where do Europe and Asia join?

Europe is part of the Asian landmass, for no sea divides it from Asia. In the east, several natural land barriers form a boundary between Europe and Asia. These barriers include the Ural Mountains, the Ural River, and the Caspian Sea. Since Europe and Asia are joined, the two together are sometimes referred to as Eurasia.

Which is Europe's longest river?

The longest river in Europe is the Volga. It flows for 2,193 feet across Russia and empties into the Caspian Sea.

Why is western Europe ice-free in winter?

Although much of the coast of Norway lies in Arctic waters, it is not ice-bound in winter. Norway, like the rest of northwest Europe, has milder winters than places in North America that are equally far north. This is because the Gulf Stream's warm waters flow across the Atlantic. The warm ocean current warms the winds blowing from the sea across western Europe, keeping winters in coastal areas (such as the United Kingdom) mild.

Europe is part of the Eurasia (Europe and Asia) landmass.

Where is Scandinavia?

Scandinavia is a region of northern Europe. The name comes from Latin, the language of the Romans. Four countries are in Scandinavia: Denmark (the most southerly), Norway, Sweden, and Iceland (an island in the Atlantic Ocean). Sometimes Finland is also included.

Where is Lapland?

Lapland is the part of Scandinavia and Finland north of the Arctic Circle. It is not a country, but takes its name from the Lapps, a people who traditionally roamed the area with their herds of reindeer. Some Lapps now live in towns and have given up their old wandering way of life.

Where is the Black Forest?

The Black Forest, or Schwarzwald in German, is a region of mountains and coniferous forest in southwest Germany. The Danube river rises there and the Rhine river flows along its western edge. The Black Forest with its dark-leaved trees is a remnant of the much larger forests that once covered most of northern Europe.

The Black Forest is one of western Europe's last remaining large forests.

Why has the Mediterranean Sea been so important?

The Mediterranean Sea has been a busy trading area for thousands of years. Civilization spread across the sea from Egypt and Mesopotamia. Greece and Rome became powerful, and later Italian city-states such as Venice grew rich from Mediterranean trade. Today the Mediterranean is still important for trade and is also a popular tourist area.

The remains of Roman buildings can be seen in many countries around the Mediterranean. This aqueduct was built in southern France.

Is all of Italy warm?

Parts of Italy have a Mediterranean climate with mild winters and hot, dry summers. The south, especially Sicily, can be very hot. However, areas of northern Italy around the Po Valley and in the Alps have cold winters.

How high are the Scottish Highlands?

The Highlands of Scotland are the highest mountains in Britain. The highest mountain, Ben Nevis, is only 4,406 feet high—small compared to the Alps. The Highlands are ancient and have been worn and weathered over many millions of years, giving them a smoothly rounded appearance.

Where is the Côte d'Azur?

In the south of France the summers are dry and hot, and there are usually many sunny winter days. The French call part of their Mediterranean coast the "sky-blue coast," or Côte d'Azur, for this reason.

Which European country has reclaimed nearly half its land from the sea?

The Netherlands. The name Netherlands means "low countries," and this part of Europe is very flat and low-lying. Sea walls called dykes hold back the sea. Pumps drain the flatlands, and a network of canals carries the water away. Large areas of marsh have been reclaimed from the sea and turned into good farmland.

Which countries share the Iberian Peninsula?

The two Iberian countries are Spain and Portugal. This square-shaped peninsula is in the southwest corner of Europe. It is surrounded by sea except at its neck, where it is joined to France. Across the neck range the high Pyrenees Mountains, a formidable natural barrier.

Where is the Camargue?

The Camargue is the delta, or mouth, of the river Rhone in southern France. It is flat, marshy country with large lagoons, such as the Étang de Vaccarès. The marshes are rich in bird life. Few people lived in the Camargue before the 1900s. It had herds of horses, bulls (used in bullfighting), and sheep. Today farmers also grow vines and rice there.

The Camargue in southern France is one of Europe's few wild places, still largely unspoilt.

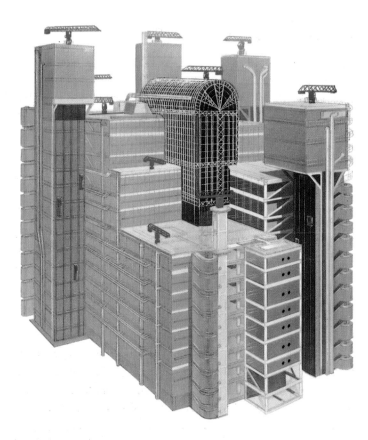

The Lloyds building in London. London has many fine buildings, old and new. It is the capital of England and the United Kingdom.

How many countries make up the British Isles?

Two: the United Kingdom and the Republic of Ireland. The United Kingdom consists of Great Britain (England, Wales, and Scotland) and Northern Ireland.

Where does the Po river flow?

The Po flows in Italy, across the broad Lombardy plain south of the Alps. It is Italy's longest river.

Where are the Carpathian Mountains?

These mountains are in central Europe. They form part of the boundary between Czechoslovakia and Poland and extend into Romania. They are lower than the Alps, with a high point of 8,711 feet, and have fewer lakes, glaciers, and waterfalls. The Carpathians in Romania are said to be the home of the legendary Count Dracula!

Where is the land of thousands of lakes?

Finland, in northwest Europe, has about 60,000 lakes and thousands of offshore islands. Europe's biggest freshwater lake is not in Finland, however. It is Ladoga, in Russia.

Where is St. Petersburg?

This Russian city was made the capital of Russia by the emperor Peter the Great in 1712. In 1914 its name was changed to Petrograd, and in 1924 it was renamed Leningrad, after the Soviet communist leader Lenin. It returned to its old name in 1991.

How long is Britain's longest river?

The rivers in Britain are not very long. The Severn, 220 miles long, is the longest.

Where are the Balkans?

The Balkans is the name of a mountain range in southeast Europe. Countries in the Balkans include Albania, Greece, Romania, and Bulgaria. To the east of the Balkans is the Black Sea, and to the south is the Mediterranean. Much of the region is wild and mountainous.

Grapes, ready for making wine, are loaded into a truck in Greece. Many people in the Balkan countries earn their living from the land.

Australia and Oceania

Where is Australasia?

Australia, New Zealand, and neighboring islands in the Pacific Ocean make up Australasia. Papua New Guinea is also included.

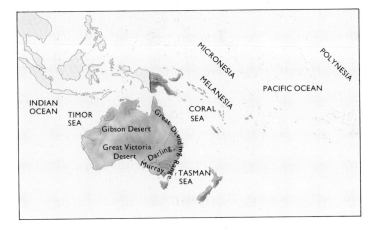

Australia is the biggest landmass in Oceania, but there are thousands of smaller islands.

How much of Australia is desert?

More than a third of Australia has less than 10 inches of rain a year and so is regarded as desert. The five biggest deserts in Australia are the Simpson, Great Victoria, Gibson, Sturt's Stony, and Great Sandy deserts. They lie in the center of the continent.

What are the Australian "bush" and "outback"?

Most Australians today live in towns and cities. They call the countryside the bush and the vast, near-empty interior of their country the outback. The outback has a few mining and farm settlements, but no large cities. Most outback farms are cattle or sheep ranches, called "stations." Some are huge, covering more than 1,000 square miles—almost as big as the state of Rhode Island.

The Australian outback. Few people live in this vast, dry area that covers much of the interior of the country.

Where is Tasmania?

Tasmania is an island about 120 miles off the coast of southern Australia. The Bass Strait separates the island from the Australian mainland. Tasmania was part of the mainland until about 12,000 years ago. It became an island when the sea rose, filling what is now the Bass Strait.

Which lake in Australia disappears?

Maps of Australia show Lake Eyre, an apparently large lake in South Australia. Yet most years the lake is dry. It fills with water only after unusually heavy rains. Most of the time it is a bed of salt. The salt forms a crust over 13 feet thick.

Where is Oceania?

Oceania is the name given to the thousands of islands scattered across the Pacific Ocean. Not all Pacific islands are part of Oceania. Indonesia, the Philippines, and Japan are part of Asia. Australia is either treated as a separate continent or is grouped with nearby islands of Oceania under the name Australasia.

Which is Australia's longest river?

Australia's rivers were a disappointment to early explorers, who hoped to find great rivers flowing out of the vast heart of the country. The longest Australian rivers are the Murray (1,600 miles) and its tributary, the Darling (1,700 miles).

For whom is Sydney, Australia, named?

In 1778 a party of British sailors and convicts landed in a bay in south Australia. They named it after Viscount Sydney, a British government minister. Sydney is now the largest city in Australia, and the harbor is famous for its bridge and its opera house (an arts center).

Are there winter sports in Australia?

Mount Kosciusko in southeast Australia is the highest mountain of the country. It is a peak in the Snowy Mountains range in the Australian Alps and is 7,310 feet high. In winter it is snow-covered and good for skiing.

How many Aborigines are there in Australia?

Today there are about 206,000 Aborigines. When Europeans first arrived in Australia in the 1700s there were at least 300,000. The Aborigines had few tools but were experts at living off the land.

Where is the Sutherland Falls?

The Sutherland Falls is one of New Zealand's many impressive waterfalls. Water plunges 1,900 feet down a mountain near Milford Sound on South Island. The falls are the fifth highest in the world.

Sheep farming is important in Australia and New Zealand.

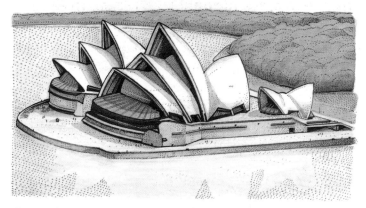

One of Australia's most famous landmarks is the opera house beside Sydney harbor.

Where are people called "Kiwis"?

New Zealanders are often referred to as "Kiwis." The kiwi, a flightless bird, has become one of New Zealand's national emblems. New Zealand's wildlife includes a number of plants and animals found nowhere else in the world. It has some of the oldest plant forms known.

Which country has more sheep than people?

One of New Zealand's most important industries is sheep farming. There are about 71 million sheep in New Zealand—that's over 20 times the number of people. Australia has even more sheep, about 135 million, compared to 15 million people.

Where in New Zealand do rocks produce steam?

The North Island of New Zealand is a region of volcanic rocks. Heat from deep beneath the Earth warms underground water, which forces its way to the surface as geysers, jets of steam, and bubbling hot springs.

Why are some Pacific islands high and others very low?

The high islands of the Pacific (such as Fiji) were made by volcanic activity on the ocean floor, which pushed up mountains. The low islands, such as Tuvalu, are coral reefs and atolls. Most are fairly small, and some of them are so low that flood waves easily sweep over them.

Where are the highest mountains in the Pacific?

The highest mountains in the Pacific region are the sea mounts that rise from the ocean floor as islands. The highest are all in New Guinea, which has several peaks over 15,000 feet high. The highest peak is Puncak Jaya in Irian Jaya (Indonesian New Guinea) at 16,503 feet.

Where could flightless birds live in peace?

Moas were large flightless birds that lived in New Zealand up to 200 years ago. New Zealand became separated from the rest of the world millions of years ago before mammals had spread over all the continents. New Zealand has only two native land mammals, both bats, which flew there. With no mammals to hunt them, flightless birds, like the moas, thrived in New Zealand. There were several kinds, of which the biggest was 10 feet high.

Which is the largest Pacific island?

New Guinea is the largest island in the Pacific and the third largest island in the world, with an area of 316,000 square miles. New Guinea and New Zealand together make up more than 80 percent of all the land in the Pacific islands. Many other Pacific islands are tiny.

Which Pacific island has the thickest forests?

Many low-lying Pacific islands have thin soils, and there is not enough rain to support many plants. New Guinea, however, is thickly forested. Rainfall is high, and many streams and rivers flow from the mountainous interior toward the swamps and grasslands of the coast.

How many islands are there in the Pacific?

No one knows exactly how many islands there are in the Pacific Ocean. There may be as many as 30,000. Some are tiny islets or coral atolls just high enough to break the ocean surface.

Where is Polynesia?

The islands of the Pacific form three main groups. These are Melanesia in the southwest Pacific; Micronesia in the northeast Pacific; and Polynesia in the central and South Pacific. Polynesia means "many islands," and this group is the largest. The distance across Polynesia from Midway Island in the north to New Zealand in the south is over 5,000 miles.

A Polynesian island. European sailors were entranced by the beauty of these islands.

Two of Australia's unusual animals

Tasmanian devil

Koala bear

North America

Where does North America start and end?

North America is the third biggest continent by land area. It stretches from Alaska in the north to Panama in the south. It includes Canada, Greenland, the United States, Mexico, Central America, and the islands of the Caribbean Sea.

Which is North America's largest country?

Canada. It covers more than 3.8 million square miles. The United States is smaller, covering 3.6 million square miles. Yet only 26 million people live in Canada compared to over 250 million in the United States.

Is Greenland part of North America?

Greenland is a self-governing part of Denmark, a country in Europe. Yet geographically this enormous island is part of North America.

North America's two biggest countries are Canada and the United States. Most of the continent lies north of the Tropic of Cancer.

Sears Tower (1,454 feet)

World Trade Centre (411 metres)

World Trade Center (1,348 feet)

The world's tallest buildings are in N. America.

Which is North America's biggest city?

Mexico City, with over 20 million people, is the biggest city in North America. The largest city in the U.S. is New York, with a population of 14 million.

Which is North America's smallest country?

Of the 23 independent North American countries, the smallest is St. Christopher and Nevis, an island state in the Caribbean. The two islands of this country, St. Kitts and Nevis, have a combined area of 101 square miles, and only 44,000 people live there. There are even smaller island states, but these are not self-governing.

What is the climate of North America like?

North America has every kind of climate. The far north is ice-covered all year round. The interior has mostly cold winters and either warm or cool summers. The southeast is warm and moist. The southwest is mostly dry with great ranges of temperature and areas of desert. In the far south, in Central America, there are hot, wet tropical forests.

Which is North America's hottest spot?

The highest temperature ever recorded in North America was 134°F at Death Valley in California, in 1913.

Where is the Yosemite Falls?

The Yosemite Falls is the highest waterfall in North America, at 2,425 feet. It is in the Yosemite National Park, Sierra Nevada (California).

Where is the world's longest frontier?

The land boundary between Canada and the United States stretches for 3,840 miles—the longest in the world.

The Canadian Rockies. The mountains, lakes, and forests of the Rockies are popular attractions for tourists.

What is the largest state in the United States?

The largest U.S. state is Alaska, which has an area of 600,000 square miles. That's three times the size of Germany.

Where is the highest mountain in North America?

In the Alaska Range, in the northwest of the continent, is Mount McKinley. It has two peaks, the highest rising to 20,320 feet. The mountain was named after William McKinley, the 25th President of the United States. Its Indian name is Denali, meaning "The High One."

Where are the Rocky Mountains?

The Rocky Mountains form the largest mountain system in North America. They extend over 3,000 miles from Canada southward into the United States. Most of the mountains were formed millions of years ago by movements of the Earth's crust.

Which river is known as the Big Muddy?

The Missouri is the second longest river in the United States. It carries with it vast amounts of mud, hence its nickname the "Big Muddy." The Indian name Missouri is said to mean "town of the large canoes."

The American badlands offer some of the most spectacular scenery in North America.

What are badlands?

In North America badlands are areas of steep hills and gullies cut by rushing streams. Soils are thin and few plants can grow there. The climate is usually dry. Sudden heavy rainstorms cause floods that wash away soil and wear down the rocks. Badlands National Park, which has a spectacular rocky landscape, is in South Dakota.

What are the Everglades?

The Everglades are subtropical swamps in the south of Florida. The Everglades cover more than 4,000 square miles. In places saw grass grows 12 feet tall. Elsewhere there are salt marshes and mangrove trees. No one lived in the swamps until the 1840s, when Seminole Indians took refuge there. Some of the swamps have been drained for farming, and part forms a national park, where visitors can see turtles, alligators, and many different kinds of birds.

What is the Canadian Shield?

This is not a defensive weapon but the biggest geological landform in Canada. It covers half the country. The Shield is an area of rocks almost 600 million years old. It has rounded hills, many lakes, and, in the south, thick conifer forests. Farther north it is too cold for trees. The Canadian Shield is an important mining region.

Where can oceangoing ships sail far inland?

Along the St. Lawrence Seaway big ships can carry cargoes from the Atlantic Ocean as far inland as the Great Lakes—a distance of over 2,000 miles. The Seaway is made up of deepened and widened stretches of the St. Lawrence River and canals. It was opened in 1959.

What is unusual about Mount Rushmore?

Mount Rushmore is a granite cliff in the Black Hills of South Dakota. Into the rock are carved four huge faces of U.S. presidents: George Washington, Thomas Jefferson, Theodore Roosevelt, and Abraham Lincoln. The head of George Washington is as high as a 5-story building. A complete figure on this scale would be over 450 feet high.

The Mount Rushmore National Memorial was completed in the 1940s. The head of George Washington (left) is 60 feet high.

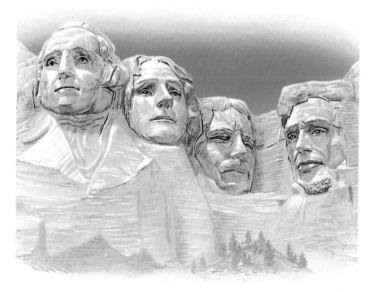

One of the main pyramids at the Mayan city of Tikal in Guatemala

Where is the Panama Canal?

The Panama Canal cuts across the Isthmus of Panama (an isthmus is a narrow neck of land). The canal is 50 miles long and was opened in 1914. Digging began in 1881, but work was abandoned after eight years because so many workers died of malaria and other diseases. In the early 1900s the U.S. took on the task, with the newly formed republic of Panama. Ships using the canal are saved a long sea journey around South America when they need to pass between the Atlantic and Pacific oceans.

What are the Antilles?

There are two main groups of Caribbean islands—the Greater Antilles and, farther east, the Lesser Antilles. The islands of the Lesser Antilles are smaller, and they include the Windward and Leeward islands.

Which is the largest island in the West Indies?

Cuba, the most westerly of the Greater Antilles islands, is the largest West Indian island. Next comes Hispaniola, which is divided into two countries: Haiti and the Dominican Republic.

Where is Central America?

Central America is the narrow land bridge joining North and South America. It extends from Guatemala and Belize in the north to Panama in the south. There are seven countries in Central America, the largest being Nicaragua.

Who built pyramids in Central America?

The native peoples of Central America developed remarkable civilizations. The Maya built great stepped pyramids. On top of each pyramid was a small temple. The Maya built cities such as Tikal, in what is now Guatemala. The great age of Mayan civilization lasted from A.D. 250 to 900.

How did the Caribbean Sea get its name?

The Caribbean Sea lies to the east of Central America. Its name comes from the Caribs, a people who lived on some of the islands of the West Indies and in South America. When Christopher Columbus sailed to America in 1492, the Spanish sailors called the sea Mar Caribe—Caribbean Sea.

Fruits such as pineapples and bananas are grown on plantations in Central America.

South America

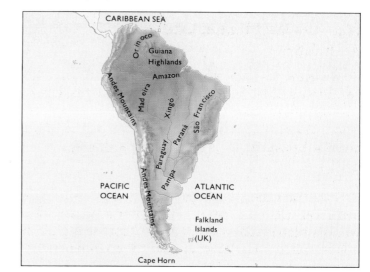

South America stretches much farther south than Africa or Australasia.

Is South America south of North America?

The South American continent is actually southeast of North America, not directly south. New York, on the east coast of North America, is farther west than Valparaiso, Chile, on the west coast of South America.

How big is South America?

South America covers an area of about 7 million square miles, so it is roughly twice as big as Canada.

Where is Cape Horn?

At the southernmost tip of South America. Most of South America lies within the tropics, yet Cape Horn is less than 600 miles from Antarctica.

What is Latin America?

This name is used to describe Mexico, Central America, and South America. Most people there speak Spanish or Portuguese—languages that developed in Europe from Latin, the language of the ancient Romans. Settlers and conquerors from Europe brought these languages to the New World.

Many Latin Americans are descended from both Indians and Europeans. The ancient traditions are "married" with customs adopted from Europe.

Who are the Native Americans?

When Christopher Columbus sailed across the Atlantic Ocean to America in 1492, he thought he had found a new sea route to Asia. He called the people he found there "Indians," thinking he was in the Indies of Asia. The native people of America had settled North and South America thousands of years before Columbus. The name "Indians" stuck, but the name "Native Americans" is more accurate.

Which are South America's most important rivers?

There are four mighty river systems in South America. They are the Magdalena, Orinoco, Amazon, and Paraná-Paraguay.

Why is Quito not so tropical?

Quito is the capital of Equador. It is only 15 miles south of the equator so it should be hot. However it is almost 10,000 feet above sea level, which means it has a mild climate.

Where is Patagonia?

Patagonia is a bleak desert region at the southern tip of Argentina. When Spanish explorers reached there in the 1500s they met local Indians who stuffed their boots with grass for extra warmth. The name Patagonia comes from a Spanish word meaning "big feet."

Which is the biggest lake in South America?

South America has fewer large lakes than other continents. The biggest lake is Lake Maracaibo (5,400 square miles) in Venezuela.

Which is the highest capital city in the world?

La Paz, the capital of Bolivia, is 12,000 feet above sea level. High in the Andes Mountains, it is the world's highest capital. Lhasa in Tibet is higher by about 160 feet, but Tibet is not now an independent country.

How big is the Amazon rain forest?

The Amazon forest is one of the wonders of the natural world. The Amazon River basin in which the rain forest grows covers about 3 million square miles. That's twice the size of India. Although much of the forest has been destroyed by logging and burning, it is still by far the biggest forest anywhere on Earth.

Indians live high in the Andes mountains. They grow crops to sell at local markets.

What is the selva?

The selva is a region of tropical rain forest in the Amazon River basin. It is one of four regions in the central plains of South America. The other three are the llanos grasslands of the north, the Gran Chaco scrub forest and the southern pampas grasslands.

The Amazon rain forest

Where do gauchos live?

Gauchos are South American cowboys. Huge herds of cattle roam the grassy plains of Brazil, Uruguay, and Argentina. The gauchos of old were wandering horsemen who rounded up wild cattle. Many later became hired ranch workers.

Why is Latin America a youthful continent?

Latin America has more than 290 million people. The population now is three times greater than 50 years ago. Many people have large families, even though they are poor. About a third of all Latin Americans are under 15 years old.

Which is the biggest city in South America?

São Paulo, in Brazil, with a population of more than seven million, is the largest South American city. However, it is not Brazil's capital. Brasília, a new city with some 400,000 people in the center of the country, replaced Rio de Janeiro as the capital of Brazil in 1960.

Is South America rich in minerals?

Yes, the continent has large reserves of metals such as copper, iron ore, lead, zinc, and gold. Venezuela is the chief South American oil producer. Bolivia has tin mines. Guyana, Surinam, and Brazil mine bauxite (aluminum ore).

South American cities often have Spanish-style plazas or squares. This is the Plaza de Mayo in Buenos Aires, the capital of Argentina.

Many South Americans live in shantytowns, squalid slums encircling the cities.

What does Cotopaxi do?

From time to time it erupts, for Cotopaxi is one of the world's highest active volcanoes. It has erupted 25 times in the past 400 years, the last time in 1975. Cotopaxi is in Ecuador and is 19,347 feet high.

Why do some South American places have Dutch names?

Many people in South America speak Spanish or Portuguese, the languages of Europeans who settled and conquered most of South America from the late 1400s. In Surinam, on the northeast coast, the official language is Dutch. Surinam was once a Dutch colony. In neighboring French Guiana and Guyana, the people speak French and English.

Which part of South America has the hottest weather?

The Gran Chaco region of Argentina. Here it can get as hot as 110°F. Most of South America has its hottest weather in January, which is a summer month south of the equator.

Where does the Orinoco River flow?

This South American river flows in a sweeping course through Venezuela in the north of the continent and empties its waters into the Atlantic. It forms the border between Venezuela and Colombia for part of its course.

Where is Sugar Loaf Mountain?

The Brazilian city of Rio de Janeiro is famous for its white sandy beaches, its carnival, and two mountain landmarks known as Sugar Loaf (1,333 feet high) and Corcovado (2,323 feet high). Sugar Loaf is a curious egg shape, and on top of Corcovado is a 100-foot-high statue of Jesus Christ.

Where is the finest natural harbor in South America?

Despite having a very long coastline, South America has few bays suitable for use as harbors. The finest natural harbor is at Rio de Janeiro in Brazil.

Where are the world's longest mountains?

The Andes stretch more than 4,000 miles along the western side of South America. They form the world's longest mountain range (not counting undersea mountains). Aconcagua in Argentina (22,831 feet) is the highest peak in the western hemisphere.

This statue of Christ stands above the harbor of Rio de Janeiro in Brazil.

La Boca district in Buenos Aires is famous for its brightly painted houses.

117

RESOURCES

What are the Earth's resources?

Ever since the first humans learned to make stone tools and burn firewood, we have been using the Earth's resources. The Earth is immensely rich in natural resources. They make life possible. Water in rivers and lakes is a resource. So too are forests and minerals. Some resources, for instance plants, are renewable: they grow again. Others, such as oil, are not. Since the industrial revolution, the demand for the Earth's resources has increased dramatically, as fuel and minerals are needed in factories. As the human population grows, even more land, water, and food are needed.

Non-renewable resources

Renewable resources

What are the oceans' resources?

The world's oceans are rich in fish, although some kinds of fish are becoming rare because too many are netted for food. The seabed contains valuable minerals, including oil beneath the rocks. Another important ocean resource for the future is power from tides and waves that can be used to make electricity. Seawater can also be made into fresh water for drinking.

What are raw materials?

People use resources to make things. We cut down trees for timber, which is used as a building material and is made into paper and furniture. The timber is a raw material. Copper is a mineral raw material. It is often mined in one country and shipped across the ocean to factories in other countries—to make electrical wiring, for example.

Why do some countries produce more food than others?

In the United States, Australia, and Europe, most farms are modern and efficient. Farmers produce more food than is needed to feed their own people. So some food can be exported (sold to other countries). Many poorer countries cannot feed their people. Farms are small and methods old-fashioned. Droughts, disease, and insect pests ruin crops, and people go hungry.

Factories and power stations in the industrialized countries consume huge quantities of fuel, such as coal and oil. These resources are nonrenewable, unlike water and timber which can be replenished.

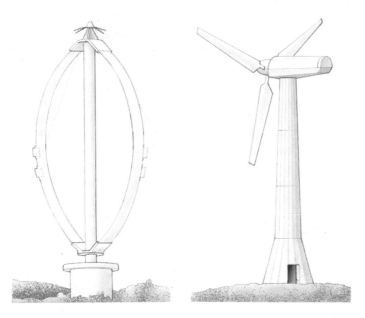

Two designs of wind generator

Is there a safe way of obtaining nuclear energy?

The world began producing electricity from nuclear power stations in the 1950s. The stations working at present control the energy produced by nuclear fission (splitting the atom). They have not proved as cheap or as safe as was hoped when the nuclear age began. But nuclear power may still have an important part to play. Vastly greater amounts of energy could be obtained from nuclear fusion (joining together atoms). Fusion happens inside the Sun and other stars and is the basis of the hydrogen bomb. The only fuels needed are deuterium (from seawater) and tritium (which can be made from an abundant element called lithium). Scientists are working toward a safe design for a waste-free fusion power system. If they succeed, the power of the Sun could help solve the world's energy problems in the 21st century.

How can we use wind power?

People have used wind power for hundreds of years in windmills. In ancient times people used windmills to pump water or grind grain. Today windmills can be used to generate electricity as well as for pumping. Windmills in California could provide 10 percent of the state's energy by the year 2000.

How does water make electricity?

The power of moving water can be harnessed to drive generators that make electricity. This is called hydroelectric power. One way to produce it is to dam a river. A lake forms behind the dam. Water from the lake is run through pipes with enormous force to drive turbines in the generating plant.

In a hydroelectric power station, engineers make use of the power of falling water. The water spins huge turbine blades to drive the electricity generator. South America gets 75 percent of its electricity from water power.

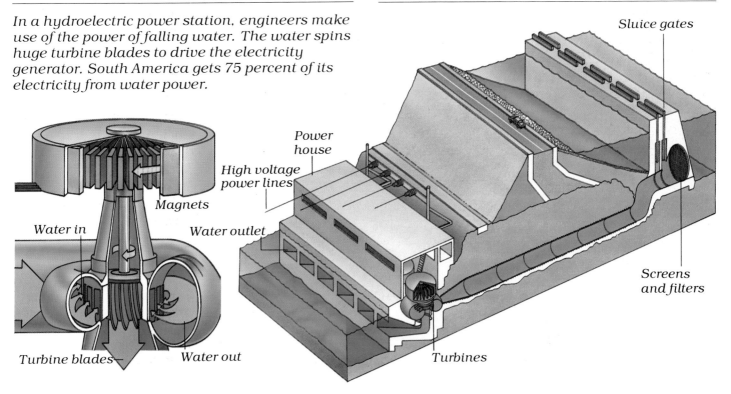

119

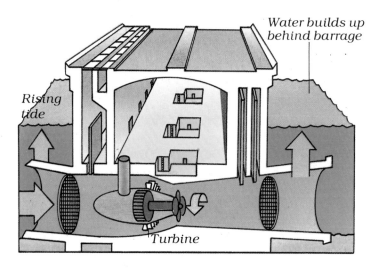

Water builds up behind barrage

Rising tide

Turbine

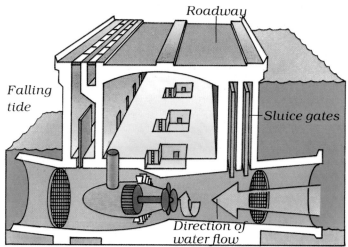

Roadway

Falling tide

Sluice gates

Direction of water flow

How can ocean tides light up our homes?

The daily movement of the ocean tides is a vast source of energy. The flow of the tides can be made to drive turbines for generating electricity. The world's first tidal power station opened on the Rance river in France in 1966.

What is solar energy?

Solar means "of the Sun." All energy comes in some way from the Sun—even the winds are driven by the Sun's heat. We can also make direct use of solar energy, for example by fitting houses with solar panels. These panels collect the Sun's warmth and use it to heat water.

In a tidal power station, the daily flow of the ocean tide drives the turbines.

What is crude oil?

Petroleum is found beneath the ground, usually as a liquid called crude oil. It also contains natural gas and solid hydrocarbons. Crude oil can be thin and watery-looking or thick and sticky, like tar. Crude oil must be refined, or processed, to change it into useful products such as fuel oil.

Which is the most valuable raw material?

Petroleum is probably the world's most important raw material. It is used for fuel. About half of the world's energy (for heating, running machines, and for transportation) comes from oil. Petroleum can also make all kinds of other substances such as plastics, which we use every day.

Where does oil come from?

Oil is found in rocks beneath every continent and beneath the oceans. However, some countries have much more oil than others. The Middle East has more than half of the world's oil. The places where oil is concentrated are called deposits. Usually only about a third of the oil in a deposit can be pumped out of the ground.

A solar energy farm. The mirrors automatically tilt as they follow the path of the Sun each day.

How was petroleum formed?

Most scientists think that petroleum was formed from the remains of tiny plants and animals that lived in the oceans millions of years ago. Oil is made up of carbon-containing substances which scientists believe must have come from living things. However, a few scientists disagree. They think oil comes from carbon-containing materials trapped inside the rocks when the Earth was formed.

An oil field in Saudi Arabia. Petroleum is the most important fuel used today.

What are hydrocarbons?

Hydrocarbons are chemical compounds made of the elements hydrogen and carbon. Crude oil (the kind found in rocks beneath the ground) is a mixture of many different hydrocarbons.

What are petrochemicals?

Petrochemicals are valuable chemicals which are made from crude oil (petroleum) or from natural gas. We need them to make many useful materials such as plastics, detergents, drugs, and fertilizers.

Where does most of the world's coal come from?

Coal is mined either from deep underground seams or from nearer the surface after the grass and trees have been stripped away. The world's two leading coal-mining countries are China and the United States.

Who uses most of the world's energy?

People in rich countries use far more of the Earth's resources and energy than people in poor countries. For example the United States uses more than 28 percent of the world's gasoline, although it has only about 5 percent of the world's population.

Where does electricity come from?

Much of the electricity we use every day is made in power stations burning oil or coal. We heat homes and factories with gas or oil from below the ground. We fill our cars, trucks, and buses with gasoline. These fuels are extracted from the Earth. They were formed millions of years ago and are nonrenewable resources: we cannot make more of them.

How much oil is produced?

World oil production is about 19 billion barrels a year. A barrel is 42 gallons. There are still about 1.5 to 2 trillion barrels of oil under the ground that can be reached and pumped out at a reasonable cost. There are other reserves in oil-bearing shales and sands, but extracting the oil would be expensive. But as oil becomes more scarce, it may be necessary to use these sources.

Coal was formed between 250 and 350 million years ago. It is found in seams, or layers, sandwiched between other rocks. The coal is extracted by mining.

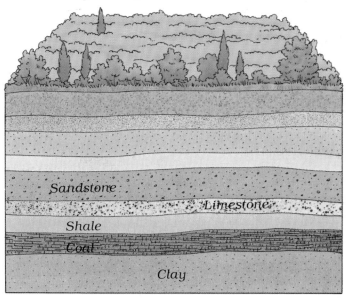

Minerals

Where did people pan for gold?

In the 1800s prospectors rushed to new gold fields in remote parts of the world. There were famous gold rushes in California (1849), in Australia (1851), in South Africa (1886), and in Canada (1896). People sought gold in streams by using a metal pan to wash specks of gold out of the gravel.

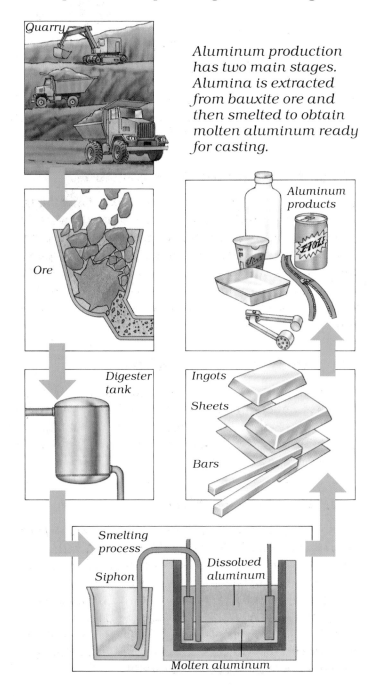

Aluminum production has two main stages. Alumina is extracted from bauxite ore and then smelted to obtain molten aluminum ready for casting.

Quarry

Ore

Digester tank

Aluminum products

Ingots

Sheets

Bars

Smelting process

Siphon

Dissolved aluminum

Molten aluminum

Why is copper useful?

People have used copper for 10,000 years. It is a soft metal and is easy to shape. It can be alloyed (mixed) with tin to make bronze. Because it is an excellent conductor of electricity, copper is widely used in electrical and telephone wiring and in electrical equipment.

Where does half the world's gold come from?

The Witwatersrand in South Africa is the richest gold field in the world. Gold was first discovered in South Africa in the 1800s, and the country now mines far more gold than any other country. The Witwatersrand mines produce more than half of the world's gold.

Where does most of the world's silver come from?

Silver is often found along with other metals, such as copper, gold, or lead. Most of the silver we use is extracted from copper and lead ores. The leading producers of silver are Mexico, Peru, Russia, and the United States.

How is aluminum made?

Aluminum is one of the most widely used metals. It is light, easily shaped, not magnetic, and does not corrode when exposed to rain and wind. Aluminum is the most plentiful metallic element on Earth but is never found on its own (pure). It is always combined with other elements. The aluminum we use is obtained from bauxite, an ore that is processed to extract the aluminum.

Where is bauxite mostly found?

Australia produces about a third of the world's bauxite. Most of the Earth's bauxite reserves are found in or around the tropics. There is enough bauxite to last for between 200 and 300 years. Processing bauxite to make aluminum uses a lot of energy. Melting down scrap aluminum is much cheaper and also means that the world's bauxite resources will last longer. It therefore makes sense to recycle as much aluminum (drink cans, for example) as possible.

Copper   Azurite   Stibnite

Graphite   Malachite   Hematite

Gold   Talc   Silver

Which country produces the most tin?

People have used tin for thousands of years. It is a soft and easily worked metal with many uses. Tin makes up only about 0.001 percent of the Earth's crust. The biggest tin producer is Malaysia.

Where is copper mined?

There are deposits of copper on every continent. The leading copper-mining countries are Chile, the United States, Canada, Russia, and Zambia. Pure copper is rarely found. Most copper comes from ores (minerals containing other elements).

How deep is the deepest mine?

The world's deepest mine is at the Western Deep Levels gold mine in South Africa. The mine is 12,392 feet deep. There are plans to dig even deeper—to more than 13,500 feet.

Where does salt come from?

The salt we put on our food is actually a chemical called sodium chloride. Salt is found in seawater and as a mineral in the ground. It can be obtained by allowing shallow pools of seawater to evaporate in the hot sun, leaving behind salt. Salt is also mined underground.

Salt can be obtained by evaporating seawater.

Minerals vary in color, hardness, and composition. Copper and silver are elements. Stibnite is a compound of sulfur and antimony.

Which stones are the most precious?

Gems are minerals used for jewelry. Diamonds, emeralds, sapphires, rubies, and opals are valuable gemstones. There are many others such as amethyst, jade, topaz, and zircon. In their natural state, most gemstones look rough and must be cut and polished to make them sparkle. Diamonds are the most valued gems because diamond is harder and more brilliant than any other mineral.

What are plastics made from?

Plastics are made from chemicals in natural materials such as coal, petroleum, limestone, salt, and water. Without these natural materials, there would be no plastics, and our lives would be very different.

What is silicon used for?

Silicon only occurs naturally in combination with other elements. It is found in rocks as silicates. Silica, or silicon dioxide, is found as sand and other minerals. Silicon is also found in the stems of some plants and in the bodies of some tiny animals. The chief use of silicon is in making chips containing microcircuits for computers and other electronic equipment. It is also used to make glass, ceramics, and photoelectric cells for cameras.

Food and Farming

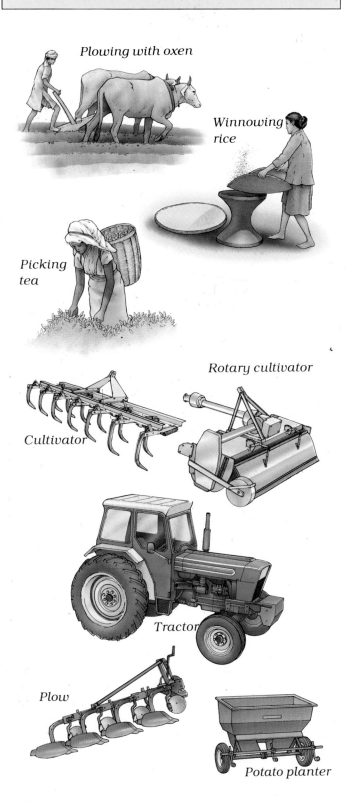

Plowing with oxen

Winnowing rice

Picking tea

Rotary cultivator

Cultivator

Tractor

Plow

Potato planter

Many farmers in the developing world still rely on simple equipment.

What are staple foods?

Staple foods are those that make up the biggest part of a person's diet. People in western countries eat a wide range of foods, but most people's diets include such foods as bread, potatoes, rice, or pasta. In Africa and Asia, people depend on staple foods such as rice, cassava (manioc), and yams. In these countries poor people may eat little else except their staple food.

What is cassava?

Cassava or manioc is an important food-plant grown in many tropical countries. People use its root to make flour, bread, and tapioca. The roots look rather like the tubers of a dahlia flower. There are many varieties of cassava.

How do subsistence farmers live?

A subsistence farmer has a small plot of land. On it the farmer grows several crops and perhaps keeps a cow or chickens. He or she can grow just enough food to feed a family for a year. In a good year, there may be some food left over to sell at the local market. Once all farmers were subsistence farmers.

Why can modern farmers grow more food?

A farmer today can grow more food than a farmer 100 years ago on the same amount of land. This is because today there are improved disease-free plants and chemicals that enrich the soil and others that kill harmful pests. However, the modern farmer grows far fewer kinds of plant than the farmer of yesterday. Main food crops such as wheat and rice are now grown on a huge scale. There are few of the local food-plants or local varieties of wheat or rice that were once common.

Does chocolate grow on trees?

Chocolate comes from a tropical tree, the cacao tree. Cacao trees are grown in western Africa, Brazil, and Malaysia. The tree first grew in South America, for we know the Maya and Aztec peoples grew cacao before Europeans began settling in the New World in the 1500s. The cacao tree has long, melon-shaped seeds. Inside are the beans that are made into the chocolate we eat.

Why do farmers use fertilizers?

Farmers add fertilizers to soil to restore nutrients and to feed plants to make them grow better. Some fertilizers are organic, made from animal dung, sewage, or other plants. Other fertilizers are made from chemicals. The most common factory-made kinds are nitrogen, phosphorus, and potassium fertilizers. Fertilizers boost harvests, helping to increase the world's food supply. Making factory fertilizers is expensive, however, and uses up valuable raw materials.

When are fertilizers used?

Farmers have always put animal manure (dung) on their fields to restore nutrients after a crop has been grown. It was in the 1800s that farmers first used chemical fertilizers. One of the first important discoveries came in 1842 when a British scientist discovered how to produce superphosphate, used as fertilizer, from rock.

What are cash crops?

A farmer who grows just one crop (such as potatoes, apples, or bananas) is growing a cash crop. When the crop is harvested, the farmer sells it for money. Farmers in some countries rely almost entirely on one such crop—such as coffee, cocoa, or tea—which is raised on large farms or plantations. People who once had their own farms often now work for wages on plantations.

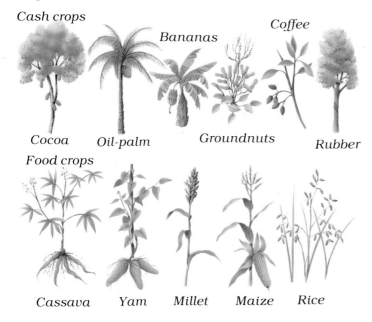

Cash crops

Cocoa Oil-palm Bananas Groundnuts Coffee Rubber

Food crops

Cassava Yam Millet Maize Rice

Farmers in Asia grow rice in flooded fields. The young rice plants need plenty of water.

Which crop grows in flooded fields?

Young rice plants are planted in a flooded field because they need lots of water to grow. The fields are surrounded by mud banks and drainage channels. The water is drained away when the rice is ready for harvesting. Rice grows best in warm, moist lands. One kind of rice, called upland rice, can be grown on dry hillsides.

Why are beans useful plants?

The beans we eat are the seeds or pods of various bean plants. Beans are very nourishing foods. They are rich in proteins, carbohydrates, and vitamins. Beans also enrich the soil with nitrogen from the air.

What is guano?

Guano is the piled-up droppings of seabirds. Islands off the coast of Peru are rich in guano, because thousands of seabirds live there. Guano makes excellent fertilizer. It is rich in nitrogen, phosphoric acid, and potash. Bat guano, from the floors of caves, is also used as fertilizer.

Some of the most important cash crops and subsistence (food) crops

Cows in a modern milking parlor. Dairy farming is important in Europe, America, and Australia.

Which country has the most cattle?

India has probably twice as many cattle as any other country—more than 275 million! However, since India's Hindu people believe the cow is a sacred animal, cattle are never killed for meat. The world's largest beef (cattle meat) producers are Brazil and the United States. There are more than 180 million cattle in Brazil, most grazing on large ranches.

What was the green revolution?

In the 1960s food scientists introduced new varieties of wheat, rice, and other crops. These gave better harvests and were developed for farmers in countries like India that had to feed huge and growing populations. By planting the new seeds and by improving their irrigation and fertilizers, some countries doubled their grain harvest. The so-called "green revolution" helped to feed some of the world's hungry people but has not solved the world food shortage.

How is grain stored?

Some of the most important food crops are cereal grains such as wheat. The wheat is cut in the fields by combine harvesters that separate the grain (the seeds) from the stalks. The grain is brought in by wagons for storage. First it is dried with hot air. Then it is piped into a large bin or silo. Farmers can store grain for many months, waiting for the price to rise.

What is dairy farming?

Dairy farmers raise cattle for their milk. Some other animals, such as horses, camels, goats, and sheep are also milked in certain countries. Cow's milk is used to make foods such as butter and cheese.

What are farm pests?

Farm pests threaten the growth or storage of farm crops. Pests include weeds, which compete with the crops for soil, air, and water, and insects, which either spread disease or eat the plants. There are also pests that affect farm animals, mainly by infecting them with diseases.

Why do farmers till the soil?

Tilling means preparing the soil for planting. First the farmer plows the soil to loosen it, kill weeds, and let in more air and water. If the soil remains in large chunks, a farmer will break it down into smaller grains by dragging a harrow across the field. The harrow works in the same way as a rake. Before planting, the soil may also be treated with weed killer and fertilizer.

Irrigation transforms an area of desert into productive farmland.

Irrigation canal

In Canada, the United States, and in Ukraine, wheat is grown on vast, flat prairies.

What are the two most important grain crops?

Wheat and rice are the most important grains. The seeds of these plants are rich in starch and so are a good source of food-energy for people and animals. Wheat is the world's chief food grain. Foods made from wheat include flour, bread, and pasta. Rice grows better than wheat in warm, wet climates. It is the main food for about half the world's people.

How is cotton produced?

Cotton, the most important of the natural fibers used to make cloth, comes from the cotton plant. The flowers of the cotton plant are white to purple-pink. When the petals fall, seed containers called bolls form. The bolls ripen and burst, making the plant look as if it is covered with fluffy snowballs. The cotton fibers are actually fine hairs growing on the skin of the seeds inside the boll. When the fibers are removed, they can be spun into lengths of yarn or thread. The yarn is then woven into cloth. Cotton-seed oil is used to make cooking oil, margarine, soap, and cosmetics.

Where does coffee come from?

Coffee is made from beans picked from a tree. The coffee tree probably grew originally in Africa. It is now grown mainly in South America and Asia. Countries that grow coffee include Brazil, Colombia, Indonesia, and Kenya. The coffee tree can grow as high as 40 feet, but is kept trimmed to only 7 to 10 feet so that the fruit can be reached easily. The berries contain two beans that are removed and then dried and roasted.

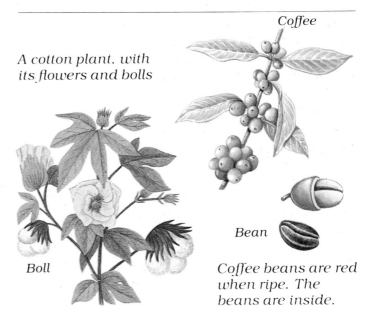

Coffee

A cotton plant, with its flowers and bolls

Boll

Bean

Coffee beans are red when ripe. The beans are inside.

127

Forestry and Fishing

What is a managed forest?

Once all forests were wild. People went into them to hunt, to gather food, or to cut wood. Much of our wood still comes from wild forests. Trees are cut down, and then the loggers move on. They do not plant new trees to replace the ones they have cut down. A managed forest is one where new young trees are planted to replace those cut for timber. A forest can be managed so that it still looks like a wild forest, with trees growing naturally. Or it can be a plantation, with trees planted in rows—good for producing timber but not very attractive to people or wildlife.

What kinds of trees are cut for timber?

The world's forests produce two kinds of timber. Softwoods come from conifer trees such as pine, fir, larch, and spruce. Hardwoods come from broad-leaved trees such as maple, oak, and walnut (which grow in cool climates) and from tropical trees such as mahogany and ebony.

Why is bamboo unusual?

Bamboo is not a tree, but a giant grass. Some kinds of bamboo grow in warm climates, and bamboo "wood" has all kinds of uses. Houses, furniture, mats, shoes, fences, scaffolding, tools, rafts, and umbrellas can all be made from bamboo. Young bamboo shoots can be eaten as a tasty vegetable. No other tropical plant has as many uses as bamboo.

Most newsprint is made from managed forests, where new trees are planted to replace those cut down.

Why do we need trees to make paper?

From trees we get wood, which has hundreds of uses. An important use is making paper, such as the newsprint on which the world's newspapers are printed. In the Western Hemisphere each one of us uses up to 600 pounds of paper or cardboard a year. Most paper is made from wood pulp (mashed-up wood).

Where do most of the fish we eat come from?

Most of the world's fish catch comes from the sea—almost 90 percent in fact. Most of these fish are caught in the open ocean by fishing boats, although an increasing quantity are raised in fish farms around the coasts. The remainder of the world's fish catch (roughly 10 percent) comes from rivers, lakes, and inland fish farms.

How can fish be farmed?

Fishing is a kind of hunting. Thousands of years ago people changed from hunting cattle or sheep to keeping them on farms. We can do the same with fish. On a modern fish farm, fish are reared in large freshwater ponds or in pens off the seacoast. The fish are fed nourishing foods to make them grow fast. Salmon and trout are farmed in this way.

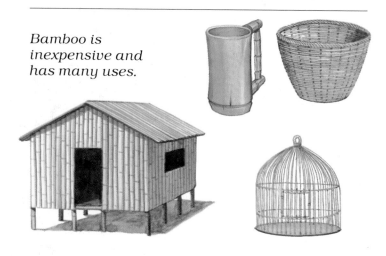

Bamboo is inexpensive and has many uses.

Why are some fish becoming harder to catch?

There are millions of fish in the sea, but people catch huge amounts. Japan catches more than 11.5 million tons of fish every year. Fishing boats now use radar and sonar (echolocation) to find fish. Their huge nets scoop up thousands of fish. Regulations limit how many fish are caught. The net holes allow small young fish to escape, to grow and breed. If too many fish are netted, fish stocks may dwindle until hardly any fish are left to catch.

What kinds of fish do we eat?

Fish is an important food in many countries, especially in Asia. The main kinds of fish caught include sardines, cod and pollack (a kind of cod), mackerel, herring, and tuna. We also eat lots of crustaceans (crabs, shrimps, and prawns) and mollusks or shellfish (oysters, clams, and mussels).

How are fish caught at sea?

Netting is the most common method of ocean fishing, although some fish are caught on lines. Fishing fleets use very large nets. There are three main kinds of net: seines, trawls, and gill or drift nets. Seines are ring-shaped nets used to encircle schools of fish. Trawls are bag-shaped nets dragged along or just above the seabed. Gill or drift nets are long wall-like nets hanging in the water.

How many fish can be netted in one haul?

Modern fishing methods are so efficient that a fishing boat can net an astonishing number of fish at one time. In 1986 a Norwegian vessel using a purse seine caught roughly 120 million fish in one catch! The catch weighed over 2,600 tons.

Fishing methods and some important food fish

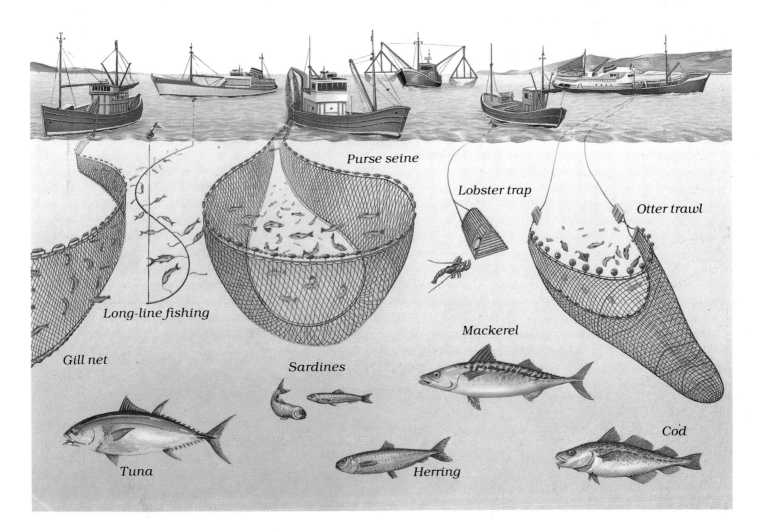

Purse seine

Lobster trap

Otter trawl

Long-line fishing

Gill net

Sardines

Mackerel

Tuna

Herring

Cod

ENVIRONMENT

What is ecology?

Ecology deals with the links between living things (animals and plants) and between them and their environment (surroundings). Scientists who study these links are called ecologists.

Is there a balance of nature?

Plants and animals depend on one another in various ways. All living things depend on their environment. This is the "balance of nature." The balance is very delicate since so many living things are involved. Upsetting one part of the structure, by people's actions for instance, can upset the whole.

What is a food chain?

A food chain is a simple way to describe how energy passes from one living thing to another. Here is one example: the grass on the North American prairie grows using energy from the Sun. Grazing animals such as prairie marmots eat the grass. Coyotes and hawks eat the marmots.

Food pyramid

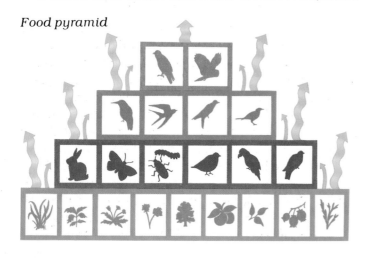

What is the biosphere?

The biosphere is where life can exist: it is the "living globe." It includes the Earth's crust (as deep down as life exists), the waters in lakes, rivers, and seas, and the air up to the height at which living things may be found.

Which are the Earth's oldest and richest living communities?

The coral reefs probably fit this category best. Most reefs are between 5,000 and 10,000 years old, but rest on dead reefs that are millions of years old. The coral reefs are as rich in species as the tropical rain forests. One reef may contain 3,000 kinds of corals, fish, crustaceans, and mollusks.

Why are some animals scavengers?

Vultures do not hunt for themselves. Instead they feed on the remains of dead animals killed by carnivores. They are scavengers. They rapidly "clean up" the animal remains, leaving only scraps of skin and bone. Scavenging insects, such as beetles, finish the task by breaking down the remains completely.

What is an ecosystem?

This is a group of living things (plants and animals) that live together in a particular place. Animals and plants of a cool forest, for example, make up one ecosystem. Animals and plants in a lake make up another.

The energy animals use to fuel their movements is lost from the food chain. Only the energy stored in body tissue is passed on.

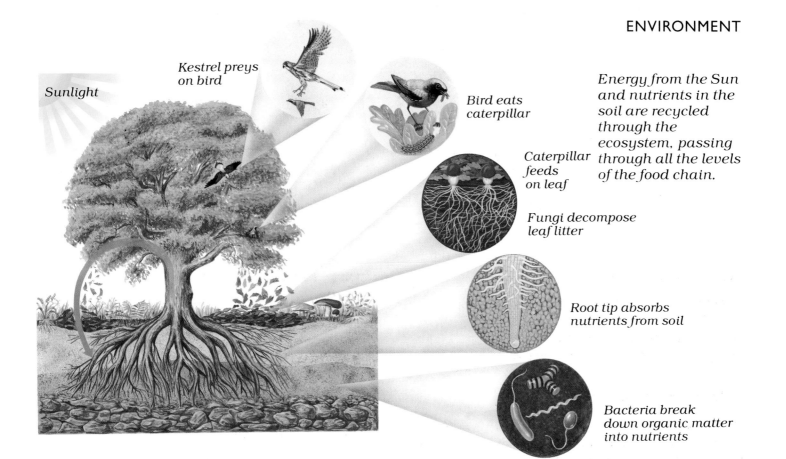

Kestrel preys on bird

Sunlight

Bird eats caterpillar

Caterpillar feeds on leaf

Energy from the Sun and nutrients in the soil are recycled through the ecosystem, passing through all the levels of the food chain.

Fungi decompose leaf litter

Root tip absorbs nutrients from soil

Bacteria break down organic matter into nutrients

What happens when there are no predators?

A predator is a hunter, catching other animals for food. Without predators the balance of nature is easily upset. For example, in the highlands of Scotland there are herds of red deer. Wolves are the natural predators of deer, but wolves in Scotland were hunted to extinction. So the numbers of deer keep on growing. Since the deer have only a certain amount of land to feed from, they would starve if there were no humans to act as "controllers" by killing a certain number of deer each year. This is called culling.

How can hungry insects exist on mountaintops?

Climbers are sometimes surprised to find beetles and spiders on high mountain peaks. What can such animals find to eat? The beetles and spiders are hunters and scavengers. They eat the insects that are blown onto the mountains by strong winds. A high mountain peak in summer might receive as much as 9 tons of insect food in this way to provide meals for the hardy mountain-climbing beetles and spiders.

What did rabbits do to Australia?

Before 1850 there were no rabbits in Australia. In that year three pairs of rabbits from Europe were released in Australia by settlers who thought they would be useful for food. However within a few years Australia was overrun by rabbits. They nibbled away all the grass, and farmers had to put up fences to keep them out. There were no natural predators such as the fox, which controls rabbit numbers in Europe. Rabbits are still a pest in Australia.

Why do some animals eat others?

The energy that supports life on Earth comes from sunlight. Plants use this energy, and some animals obtain it by eating the plants. Plant-eating animals (herbivores) are preyed on by meat-eaters (carnivores). The carnivores control the numbers of herbivores. They prevent the herbivores from becoming so numerous that they eat all the available plant food, and cause mass starvation. This helps to maintain the balance of nature. For example, if the bird population rises, the caterpillar population will fall. The birds will therefore die or move on in search of fresh food supplies. The caterpillar population will then increase, and the balance is restored.

Conservation

Why is it a tragedy to lose one species of animal or plant?

By the year 2050 scientists fear that as many as half of the Earth's animal and plant species could be extinct. Yet each species is a storehouse of genetic resources. To lose one species can be a tragedy. For example, drugs made from the rosy periwinkle, a plant of the Madagascar forest, are now used to help treat children suffering from leukemia (a form of cancer). If this one plant had died out, its medical value would never have been known.

Why are island animals in the most danger?

Island animals have evolved in isolation, often with few predators and little competition from rival species. Some island birds, for example, gave up flying. They did not need to fly because there were no rats, weasels, or foxes to prey on them. Such animals survived well until people arrived by boat, bringing dogs, cats, and rats. Many were then hunted until they died out.

Why is Madagascar so special?

The island of Madagascar has about 10,000 plant species, and 8,000 of these are found nowhere else. It has almost 200 kinds of birds, about half of which live nowhere else. It has two-thirds of the world's chameleons and all the 30 surviving species of lemurs. Because it is an island, life on Madagascar has evolved separately from that of the rest of Africa.

The radiated tortoise from Madagascar

Gorillas need undisturbed forest to live in.

Are gorillas a national asset?

Rare animals can be saved only if local people benefit from their survival. In Rwanda, a small, poor country in central Africa, foreign tourists come to see the rare gorillas. The money the tourists spend is a useful addition to Rwanda's national income. Other countries can benefit from preserving wildlife as tourist attractions.

Is there more life in some places than others?

Some environments are very rich in living things. Tropical rain forests have the greatest mix of species. A ten-mile-square patch of forest may be home to more than 2,000 plant species, 400 kinds of birds, 150 butterflies, 100 reptiles, and 60 amphibians. There are so many insects that no one can count them!

Why do animals die out?

When a species dies out, it becomes extinct. In the Earth's history there have been periods of mass extinctions—when the dinosaurs disappeared about 65 million years ago, for example. In the last 200 years people have become the most serious threat to animals. By destroying their habitat (the places in which they live) or by killing the animals themselves, humans have already killed off over 300 animal species since the year 1600. Many more are in serious danger.

Were there nature reserves in past times?

Hunting parks and forests reserved for kings were an ancient form of nature reserve. Animals were protected (except from the royal hunters), and people were kept out. In Holland a wooded nature reserve was set aside by the Prince of Orange and the state government in 1576. The first true national park set up to protect nature and wildlife for everyone to enjoy was the Yellowstone National Park in Wyoming. It was founded in 1872.

What is the wildlife trade?

Millions of wild animals are trapped or killed each year. Some are caught alive to be sold as pets. Birds and tropical fish in particular are in danger from this trade, but so are snakes and monkeys, among others. Many more wild creatures are killed for their skins. Rhinos are shot by poachers so that their horns can be made into dagger handles. Elephants have been hunted for their tusk ivory. Some of this trade is legal but much of it is illegal, carried on secretly by poachers and smugglers.

How did the arrival of humans on Hawaii affect wildlife there?

When Polynesian settlers reached the Hawaiian Islands 1,500 years ago, they swiftly killed off about 40 species of birds, either by hunting or by destroying the birds' habitat.

Why is the U.S. grass greener?

Scientists have found that at the U.S.-Mexican border, the grass grows greener on the U.S. side. The climate is slightly warmer on the Mexican side because cattle grazing is less strictly controlled in Mexico. If too many cows graze on the pasture, the soil is exposed to the sun, and it heats up and dries out. The temperature on the Mexican side can be 7°F higher than in the U.S. because Mexico has no laws to limit the numbers of cattle grazing. This is why the grass grows greener on the U.S. side.

Where did Peru's anchovies go?

The anchovies went into fishing nets. The sea off Peru once held a quarter of all the world's anchovies. So many were caught that by the 1970s there were hardly any left. Fishermen were out of work, and the numbers of anchovies have never recovered.

Which Asian country is the most forested?

Perhaps surprisingly, the answer is Japan. About 66 percent of Japan is covered by forest. In China, which is much bigger than Japan, only about 11 percent of the land is forested.

Much of the interior of Japan is mountainous and covered with forest.

Pollution

Smog in Los Angeles

What causes air pollution?

Most air pollution is caused by burning, which releases gases and smoke. Clear air becomes murky and smelly and can become poisonous. Car engines give off the waste gases carbon monoxide and nitrogen dioxide. These gases damage plants and people's lungs. Factory chimneys pour out smoke, gas, and tiny particles of solid waste.

Why is pollution a problem?

Human beings have always dirtied their surroundings, with rubbish or smoke for example. The problem now is that so many more people dirty and spoil our world in many ways. We release gases and smoke into the air. We pour poisons into water. We damage the soil with chemicals. We drop litter, cover fields with concrete, and make a lot of noise. Pollution can make people ill and kills wildlife.

What dirties the air?

The air in a big city is made dirty by a mixture of things. These pollutants include sulfur and nitrogen dioxide from power stations and factory chimneys. Vehicle exhausts and oil refineries give off hydrocarbons. Heavy metals such as lead come from cars, smelters, and factories, while chemicals are given off as waste by chemical industries.

What is smog?

Smog is a mixture of pollutants that causes a fog-like haze over a city. It is worst in places with lots of cars or factories close to the city center. These give off chemical fumes and smoke. Cities with bad smog include Mexico City, Los Angeles, Athens, Beijing, Tehran, and Lagos. Breathing smoggy air is said to be as harmful as smoking 40 cigarettes a day.

Can we beat city air pollution?

Since the 1970s cities have tried new ways to fight smog. In Los Angeles all cars must be fitted with catalytic converters which scrub clean the exhaust gases from the engine. Even with unleaded gasoline and cleaner engines, cars still cause air pollution. Some cities have restricted areas, for example no cars are allowed in the center of Florence, Italy, during daylight.

The main sources of pollution

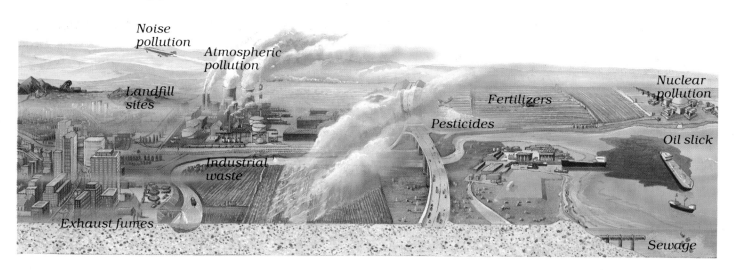

Noise pollution

Atmospheric pollution

Landfill sites

Industrial waste

Exhaust fumes

Fertilizers

Pesticides

Nuclear pollution

Oil slick

Sewage

Is there an alternative to the car?

Public transportation, including cheap or free buses and trains, might be used instead of the car in cities. However, it is unlikely that cars will disappear completely from city streets. Electric cars with batteries give off no exhaust fumes, so they may one day replace gasoline-driven cars in cities.

What started warming the Earth?

In the past the Earth's climate warmed and cooled over millions of years. Since the 1700s, however, people have caused a far more rapid climate change. The industrial revolution that began in the 1700s brought factories, railways, fast-growing cities, and motor vehicles. Carbon dioxide and other gases have been poured into the atmosphere from burning fuels such as coal and oil in factories, homes, and vehicles. This change, brought about by the industrial revolution, is warming the Earth.

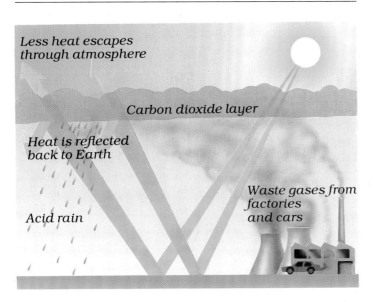

The greenhouse effect is caused by a buildup of gases such as carbon dioxide in the atmosphere.

What is the greenhouse effect?

Most scientists now agree that the Earth is getting warmer. This is happening because carbon dioxide and other gases in the atmosphere act like glass in a greenhouse. They let the Sun's rays though, but trap some heat that would normally be radiated from the ground and into space. This trapped heat is warming the Earth and altering the climate.

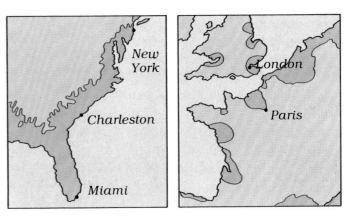

The maps show how a rise in sea level would affect areas of Europe and the U.S.

Why will sea levels rise?

As the world warms up, more of the ice around the North and South poles will melt. During the next century, the level of the sea could rise by 3 feet or more. This could flood low-lying countries such as the Maldive Islands in the Indian Ocean and cover about a third of Bangladesh. Millions of people would lose their homes.

What would a warmer Earth be like?

We still do not know what effect global warming will have on the Earth. Lands that at present have cold winters, such as Canada, may well become warmer. Warm countries such as Greece may suffer drought. Lands such as Ethiopia, which are already very dry and dependent on seasonal rains, could become deserts.

What are CFCs?

In the 1970s scientists discovered that something unusual was happening to the ozone layer over the South Pole. The ozone layer (which shields us from harmful ultraviolet radiation from the Sun) had become thinner and the "hole" over the Antarctic was getting bigger. The cause was identified as a group of gases called chlorofluorocarbons or CFCs, which are used in aerosols such as hairsprays, in refrigerators, and in making packaging. Scientists warned that CFCs were a threat to the ozone layer and should not be used. Manufacturers are switching to other gases, but some countries continue to use CFCs. It is hoped that eventually all countries will stop using CFCs altogether.

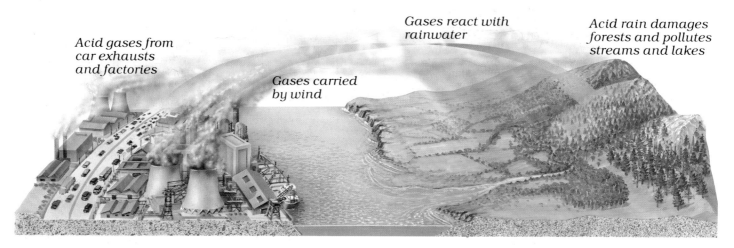

Acid gases from car exhausts and factories

Gases carried by wind

Gases react with rainwater

Acid rain damages forests and pollutes streams and lakes

What is acid rain?

Acid rain contains acids from polluted air. All rainwater is naturally slightly acidic, but acid rain damages lakes and forests. Factories in industrial countries send out chemicals into the air. Clouds containing the acid-making chemicals are blown over neighboring countries, affecting them as well.

When did the nuclear age begin?

In 1942 scientists at the University of Chicago started up the world's first nuclear reactor. In 1956 Calder Hall in Britain became the first large nuclear station to produce electricity. The nuclear age seemed to promise unlimited amounts of cheap power.

Acid rain is caused by air pollution. Waste gases react with rainwater, and acid rain falls.

Why is nuclear power dangerous?

The massive power of a nuclear reaction can be used for destruction (in a bomb) or for peaceful purposes. Controlled nuclear energy can produce electricity more cleanly than a coal-burning power station. But it also produces a deadly poisonous waste, and there is the added danger of a nuclear accident that could spread harmful radioactivity over large areas of the Earth.

What happened at Chernobyl?

In 1986 a nuclear reactor in the Soviet power station at Chernobyl overheated during a test and caught fire. The fire burned for ten days. The reactor began to melt, and radioactive gases escaped into the air. More than 130,000 people were evacuated from their homes. More than 30 died, and thousands of people will almost certainly become ill in the future because they were affected by the radiation. The damaged reactor was sealed in concrete.

Why is nuclear waste difficult to get rid of?

Nuclear power stations produce waste that stays deadly poisonous for hundreds of years. The waste has to be stored in sealed containers. Some people think it is safe to bury it underground or on the seabed. Others disagree. The waste could also be fired in rockets to outer space. But this would be very costly, and if a single rocket were to blow up accidentally, the radioactive waste would pollute the entire planet.

A nuclear reactor

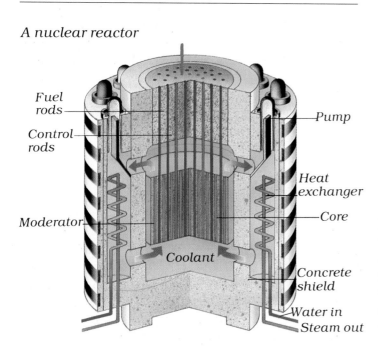

Fuel rods

Control rods

Moderator

Coolant

Pump

Heat exchanger

Core

Concrete shield

Water in

Steam out

Will nuclear power still be used a hundred years from now?

Perhaps, but not on the scale once imagined. There are more than 400 reactors producing electricity around the world. Rising costs and fears about the safety of nuclear power have now made countries halt or slow down their nuclear programs. A few countries, such as France, rely heavily on nuclear power but have found that it is not as cheap as was once hoped. Old nuclear stations are being closed down and not being replaced.

What is renewable energy?

This is the energy we can get from water (hydroelectric power), from wind (windmills), and from the oceans (tidal barrages). It is renewable because unlike coal, gas, and oil, it will never run out. We can use these energy sources over and over again.

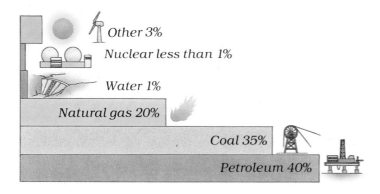

Petroleum and coal supply most of our power.

What happens to our garbage?

Most of the garbage we throw away is dumped into holes in the ground or discharged into the sea. In some countries it is burned in incinerators. Only a small amount of it is recycled, or treated so that the materials in it (paper, glass, metal, and plastics, for example) can be reused.

Why are plastic ring-packs harmful?

Even harmless-looking bits of rubbish can be dangerous to wildlife. The plastic holders used on packs of drinks cans can act as snares if carelessly thrown away. An animal that pokes its head through a loop is trapped for life and may even strangle itself. All litter should be put in trash cans.

Much of this household waste could be recycled to make useful products.

Which are "greener": plastic or paper bags?

About 40 percent of the plastics we use go into packaging. Plastic bags are given away in supermarkets everywhere. Some people think paper bags would be better. But German scientists have found that making paper bags actually produces twice as much air pollution and uses 200 times as much water. So plastic bags are "greener," if reused.

Does plastic ever rot away?

Waste paper and wood rot away in time, although scientists have dug up 40-year-old newspapers from rubbish heaps and found they are still readable! Most plastics take a very long time to decay. Scientists have invented a degradable plastic made from sugar, which is digested by bacteria in the soil. Another kind of degradable plastic breaks down when exposed to sunlight.

What nearly killed off the peregrine falcon?

The peregrine falcon is the fastest of all hunting birds. It became rare in the 1960s because of the insect-killing chemical called DDT. The DDT poison got into the soil and therefore into the food chain. Eventually it found its way into the peregrines (that ate pigeons that ate grain that grew in poisoned soil). The peregrines then laid thin-shelled eggs that did not hatch. Since DDT has been banned in many countries, the peregrine has been saved.

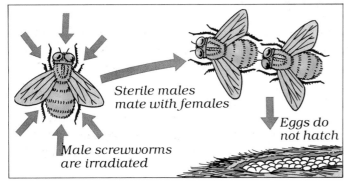

The screwworm fly was wiped out of Libya using biological control.

How can fertilizers kill fish?

Fertilizers are good for soil—in small quantities. If too much fertilizer is put into soil it can cause problems. Rain may wash the soil and the chemicals into lakes and rivers. The food-rich soil enriches the water, so algae (small plants) grow too quickly. When algae die, the waste left behind decays and uses up oxygen in the water. This can leave a lake or river dead or dying, without enough oxygen to support fish and other living things.

Pesticides sprayed on crops can get into the food chain and harm people and animals.

What is biological control?

Use of artificially produced chemicals to kill pests that attack plants or animals can leave harmful substances in the atmosphere or soil. It is often possible to fight insect pests by setting their natural predators such as wasps or beetles against them. This is known as biological control.

What happened to the screwworm?

In Libya it died out, much to farmers' relief. The screwworm is the grub of a fly. The fly lays eggs in wounds on warm-blooded animals, including humans. The grub hatches and eats its victim's flesh, often killing the unfortunate animal. Scientists controlled this pest biologically. They released a trillion sterile male flies (treated so they could not reproduce). The sterile flies mated with local female flies, which laid eggs that did not hatch. In a short time, the screwworm fly was practically extinct in Libya.

How can wild rice give us more food?

The cereals we grow today, such as wheat and rice, were developed from wild grasses. These modern cereals give much more food. But they can also suffer from pests and diseases. If farmers grew only one or two varieties of wheat, they could lose all their crop to disease. So it is important to save wild cereals as a genetic "bank." Many of the wild plants resist diseases and pests. By crossbreeding these hardy wild plants with high-yielding farm plants, farmers can grow more crops.

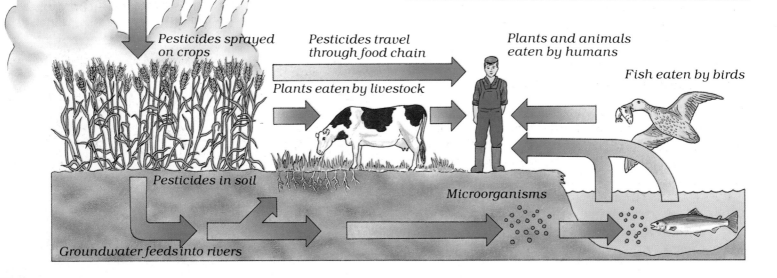

Aluminum cans

Paper

Glass

Water

Lead

Organic waste

Aluminum foil

Recycling is a sensible way to make the most of the Earth's resources.

Why was the Earth more smoggy than usual in 1990?

After the Gulf War of 1990 more than 700 oil wells in Kuwait were left blazing. They had been deliberately set on fire. Oil was also spilled into the sea, killing marine life. Fighting the oil well fires was a mammoth task, tackled by experts from all over the world. The last wells were put out by firefighters late in 1991. Smoke from the oil wells enveloped the planet. Astronauts orbiting the Earth in the space shuttle Atlantis saw that the Earth below looked smog-shrouded, because of the soot and smoke from the burning oil drifting in a cloud away from Kuwait.

Can volcanoes affect climate?

The smoke and ash from a volcano pours out into the atmosphere to form clouds. The clouds can blot out the Sun and so cool the Earth. In 1783 a volcano eruption in Iceland caused constant fog over Europe and North America. The winter that followed was colder than normal. The dust clouds produced by the eruption of Mount Pinaturbo in the Philippines in 1991 blotted out some sunlight. When volcanoes do this, the Earth cools slightly.

Why recycle paper?

Saving paper does not save endangered trees. The paper industry grows trees for paper-making, just as a grain farmer grows wheat. However, recycling paper is still sensible since it saves energy. Recycled paper production uses half as much energy as making paper from new wood and only a third as much water. In addition the paper we throw away in dumps rots slowly and gives off methane gas, which contributes to global warming.

What causes pollution of the seas?

Millions of tons of rubbish end up in the seas, so much that some small seas such as the Aral Sea and the Mediterranean Sea are now "dying." About 44 percent of ocean pollution comes from waste poured directly into the seas; about 30 percent from air pollution; 12 percent from ships; and the rest from dumping rubbish.

What causes an oil slick?

Every year more than three million tons of oil is spilled into the sea. About a third of this is washed out of the tanks of oil tankers before they reload. A tanker accident, such as the *Exxon Valdez* disaster in Alaska in 1989, can cause terrible harm to the marine environment. The oil forms a huge slick, or patch, on the water which may wash ashore, fouling beaches and killing thousands of seabirds, fish, and other animals.

The Exxon Valdez *oil tanker spilled 38,000 tons of oil off the coast of Alaska, killing thousands of birds and other sea animals.*

WHO?

Who was Alfred Wegener?

Alfred Wegener (1880–1930) was a German scientist. He suggested that because the outlines of America and Europe/Africa look similar, they may have been joined together before drifting apart. Wegener was thus one of the first people to put forward the idea of continental drift, now generally accepted by scientists.

Who are mestizos?

Mestizos are people of mixed American Indian and European origin. In South America many people are mestizos.

Who was Sir Charles Lyell?

Sir Charles Lyell (1797–1875) is known as one of the founders of modern geology. He became president of the British Geological Society in 1835. Lyell invented the names such as Eocene, Miocene, and Pliocene, which are still used to describe long periods of geological time.

Who first climbed Mount Everest?

The first people to stand on the summit of Mount Everest were a New Zealander, Edmund Hillary, and a Nepalese Sherpa, Tenzing Norgay. They were members of the Commonwealth Everest expedition of 1953. Several earlier expeditions had tried and failed to reach the summit. Since 1953, numerous ascents of Everest have been made, including climbs by people without using oxygen breathing apparatus.

Who led the first expedition to cross Australia?

Robert O'Hara Burke, an Irish explorer, was the first to cross Australia. His expedition set off from Melbourne in 1860. Four men (Burke, Wills, Grey, and King) went on ahead and reached northern Australia in 1861, almost making it to the Gulf of Carpentaria. Only King returned alive, his companions having died of exhaustion and hunger.

Who were the first people to stand at the South Pole?

Roald Amundsen of Norway and his four companions were the first to reach the South Pole on December 14, 1911.

Who were the first Europeans to settle in Canada?

Vikings or Norsemen led by Leif Ericsson sailed to the shores of eastern Canada in about A.D. 1000. Small Norse settlements may have survived there until the 1300s.

Who was the first European to cross the Sahara?

Rene Caillé of France made this journey in 1828, visiting Timbuktu on the way. He traveled disguised as an Arab in a camel caravan.

Who drew the first maps of the bottom of the Atlantic Ocean?

Matthew Fontaine Maury (1806–1873), a U.S. Navy officer and one of the founders of the science of oceanography, drew these maps for the first time. He drew charts of the Atlantic, Pacific, and Indian oceans and drew a cross section of the Atlantic seabed to show that it was possible to lay a trans-Atlantic telegraph cable.

Who landed on Mount Ararat?

According to the Bible, Noah landed there, after the Flood. The mountain on which the ark settled as the waters went down is in modern Turkey and is also known as Buguk Agri. It is 17,011 feet high.

Who was David Livingstone?

Livingstone (1813–1873) was a Scottish missionary and explorer of Africa. He made several epic journeys into the heart of Africa, braving disease and the hostility of slave traders. In 1871 he had a famous meeting with Henry Morton Stanley, who had been sent to find Livingstone, from whom nothing had been heard for years. Livingstone was a brave explorer. When Livingstone died his servants carried his body 1,400 miles to the coast. He is buried in Westminster Abbey in London.

Who invented the Celsius thermometer scale?

Anders Celsius (1701–1744), a Swedish astronomer invented this scale in 1742. The Celsius scale (sometimes known as the centigrade scale) is now used worldwide. On this scale water freezes at 0 degrees and boils at 100 degrees (at normal atmospheric pressure).

Who was Alfred Russel Wallace?

Wallace (1823–1913) was a British naturalist and traveler in Southeast Asia. Like Charles Darwin, Wallace thought that animals and plants had evolved, by the "survival of the fittest." He and Darwin made public their ideas about evolution in 1858.

Who are indigenous peoples?

Indigenous peoples are the original inhabitants of a place—such as the San of southwest Africa, the Native Americans of Brazil, the Pygmies of western Africa, the Inuit of Canada, and the Aborigines of Australia.

Who was the first European to sail across the Pacific Ocean?

The first European to cross the Pacific was Ferdinand Magellan of Portugal. He led five ships that set out in 1519 to sail around the world. Magellan was killed in the Philippines before the voyage ended. Only one ship returned, in 1522.

Who were the first geologists?

Ancient and medieval scientists knew little of the Earth's structure and how it changes. They did, however, build up a body of knowledge about products of the Earth such as minerals, precious stones, metals, crystals, and chemicals. Geology as a branch of science did not really get going until the 18th and 19th centuries.

Who was Louis Agassiz?

Agassiz (1807–1873) was one of the first great geologists. He was born in Switzerland, but he became a professor of zoology and geology at Harvard University in 1848.

Who were Lewis and Clark?

Meriwether Lewis and William Clark were American explorers. Guided by friendly Indians, they led an expedition to the west coast in 1804. Lewis and Clark were the first white explorers to cross the American West. They traveled by canoe up the Mississippi River, crossed the Rocky Mountains, and reached the Pacific Ocean in 1805.

Who built the Panama Canal?

The Panama Canal cuts across the isthmus of Panama. (An isthmus is a narrow neck of land.) The Canal is 50 miles long. Ships using it are saved the long sea journey from the Atlantic to the Pacific around South America. The Panama Canal was built by American engineers and opened in 1914.

Who first studied fossils?

The first people to study fossils seriously were 17th century scientists such as Robert Hooke (1635–1703). Hooke believed that fossils were the remains of creatures and plants, many of which must have died out since they looked very different from any species alive today.

Who first explored the New World?

The first people to explore the New World, or the Americas, were Asian wanderers who journeyed into Alaska and then southward into what is now Canada and the United States. These people traveled on foot and by boat and were the ancestors of the American Indians.

Who was Louis Leakey?

Louis Leakey (1903–1972) discovered the remains of the humanlike *Australopithecus* in Africa, which lived over 2 million years ago. His wife, Mary, and son, Richard, also made important discoveries. Mary Leakey found human footprints (of two adults and a child) made 3.7 million years ago.

Who wrote a book about minerals in 1261?

Albertus Magnus (about 1200–1280), a German who was both a churchman and scientist, was the author of the Book of Minerals. In this book Albertus listed about 100 minerals.

WHAT?

What sort of cloud produces steady rain?

Low, grey, sheetlike clouds called nimbostratus cause continuous rain.

What are angiosperms?

Flowering plants with covered seeds are called angiosperms. They have been the dominant plants on Earth since the Cretaceous period, beginning some 138 million years ago.

What are the Earth sciences?

Geology includes the study of rocks, earthquakes, volcanoes, and fossils. Meteorology is the study of the atmosphere and weather. Oceanography covers the waves, tides, currents, trenches, and ocean life. Paleontology is the study of plant and animal fossils.

What is Project Tiger?

India has 18 reserves where some 1,300 tigers are protected. There are about 4,300 tigers in India, far fewer than fifty years ago, but the numbers are increasing. Like all big hunters tigers need a large territory. Project Tiger was set up to preserve areas where tigers can live and hunt without human interference.

What is the largest gulf?

The largest gulf is the Gulf of Mexico, which covers an area of 596,000 square miles.

What is the greatest depth of the Atlantic Ocean?

In the Puerto Rico Trench the Atlantic reaches a depth of 30,400 feet.

What happens to loess?

It gets blown by the wind. Loess is a fertile, fine dust or silt that is deposited by winds on lands in central Asia, Europe, and North America.

What is lignite?

A low-grade, brownish black kind of coal. Lignite is a variety halfway between peat and black coal.

What is a marine animal?

An animal that lives in the sea is a marine animal. Marine means "of the sea" and comes from the Latin word for sea, *mare*. Marine animals include many invertebrates such as worms and mollusks, as well as fish and sea mammals such as seals, dolphins, and whales.

What is the ocean ooze made of?

The abyss (the ocean bottom) is covered with oozes (sediments). The material in the ooze is volcanic dust or the remains of dead ocean animals.

What makes a pass?

A pass is a low, narrow gap through a mountain range. It is usually the result of erosion. Passes allow travelers to cross mountains that are too high or difficult to climb.

What is shale?

It is a kind of sedimentary rock found in layers and made of compressed clay.

What is a catchment area?

This is the area from which a river draws its water, usually on high ground. Rain falls over hills and mountains and feeds springs that flow downhill to become rivers.

What is amber?

Amber looks like a yellowish brown stone but is actually the hardened remains of the sap or resin of a long-dead conifer tree.

What is the Great Karoo?

The interior of South Africa forms a saucer-shaped plateau. Around the plateau the land descends in steps to the ocean. Two such steps are the Great and Little Karoo in southern Cape Province. These are plateaus surrounded by mountains.

What is subsidence?

Subsidence is the sinking of part of the Earth's surface. Subsidence can be caused naturally by movements of rocks beneath the surface. It can also be the result of human activity, such as deep mining.

What are buttes?

These are flat-topped hills, common in the western United States in areas such as Monument Valley, in Utah, a favorite location for Western films.

What does alpine mean?

The word alpine is used to describe any high mountains and their vegetation, wildlife, and climate.

What is a discontinuity?

A discontinuity is a layer within the Earth where the speed of travel of seismic (shock) waves changes.

What is an anticline?

This is an archlike fold in rock layers. It is produced by pressure in the Earth's crust.

What is big bluestem?

This is a tall grass over 10 feet high that grows on the prairies of North America. It is often called turkeyfoot, because its flowers grow in clusters that look like a bird's foot. Altogether there are about 200 kinds of bluestem grasses.

What are gene banks?

Wild plant and animal communities provide a pool of genetic resources that may be useful at some future time for improving plants and animals already used by humans. Seeds from wild plants are stored in "banks" so that they may be used in future plant-breeding programs.

What were creodonts?

These extinct mammals were carnivores. They evolved into various forms—some were like dogs, others like cats, hyenas, and bears. But they were not related to these modern animals.

What is a levee?

This is a bank of earth and mud that builds up on the floodplain on either side of a river. Artificial levees or embankments are built to prevent rivers from flooding farmland and towns. In ancient Egypt, the pharaohs ordered embankments to be built along the left bank of the Nile River. In the United States engineers have built a massive system of levee embankments along the Mississippi River. These flood defenses were begun in the 1700s and now include some 3,000 miles of levees.

What are cetaceans?

Whales, dolphins, and porpoises are cetaceans. These mammals are so well adapted to life in the oceans that they can no longer live on land.

What is the hydrosphere?

The hydrosphere is all the water in and around the Earth. It includes rivers, lakes, oceans, ice at the poles, and water vapor in the atmosphere.

What is plate tectonics?

The theory of plate tectonics explains the way in which the Earth's crust moves. The crust and the upper mantle beneath are made up of seven huge rigid plates and about the same number of smaller plates. The slow movement of these plates causes the crust to fold and reshape. It builds mountains and causes earthquakes.

What are cays?

Cays are small, low islands. They are usually sandy and rest on a coral platform. A severe storm may wash the sea over the whole island. Many Caribbean islands are called cays or keys.

What is the Gironde?

The Gironde is a long river estuary in western France formed by the rivers Dordogne and Garonne, as they empty their waters into the Bay of Biscay.

What is quartz made of?

Quartz is the crystalline form of silicon dioxide and is the hardest of the common minerals.

What is potassium used for?

Potassium is a common element in many minerals. About 95 percent of the potassium we use goes into fertilizers.

What is cloning?

Cloning is a way of reproducing plants or animals by manipulation of their body cells, to produce exact copies of one parent, either male or female.

What happened to the sea cow?

Steller's sea cow was a large sea mammal, similar to, but much bigger than, the manatee. It lived in the Arctic. Sadly these peaceful creatures were hunted to extinction in just 27 years, from 1741 (when they were discovered) to 1768.

What is the oldest living species of tree?

During the Mesozoic era there flourished in many parts of the world a group of plants called ginkgos. These were deciduous trees with broad, subdivided leaves. The living maidenhair tree, Ginkgo biloba, is the only one of these plants that survives to this day. Fossil leaves identical to those of Ginkgo biloba are found in Triassic rocks 200 million years old.

What is wind chill?

Wind chill is a measure of how cold a wind can make a person feel. Our bodies feel colder on a windy day at low temperatures than they do on a calm day at the same temperature.

What kind of trees grow in savanna?

The scattered trees that grow in tropical grassland or savanna need to be able to survive long, hot, dry seasons. Baobab and acacia trees are typical African savanna trees.

What are monotremes?

Monotremes are egg-laying mammals, such as the echidna, or spiny anteater, and the duck-billed platypus of Australia. These animals have reptile-like body structures, but unlike reptiles they are hairy, and females feed their young on milk from their bodies.

What are sea grasses?

Sea grasses are land plants that have returned to the oceans. They grow in shallow waters in cool and warm oceans. Sea grass beds are very rich in fish.

What kinds of plants live in Antarctica?

Antarctica is too cold for most plants. There are only two flowering land plants in Antarctica. The other plants there are mosses and lichens.

What is an island arc?

A curving chain of islands associated with an ocean trench or with volcanic activity forms an island arc. The islands of Japan are an example.

What does the name Chile mean?

Chile is a country in South America. Its name comes from the language of the Araucanian Indians of the region. It means "the best on Earth," because part of the country is very fertile.

What does "paleo" mean?

"Paleo" means old or ancient. So paleontology, for example, is the study of fossils of ancient life. The Paleozoic is the era of ancient life.

What is measured on the Mohs' scale?

This scale measures the hardness of minerals. Diamond, the hardest mineral, scores 10 on the Mohs' scale. Talc, which can be crushed by your fingernail, scores 1.

What is CITES?

These initials stand for the Convention on International Trade in Endangered Species. Nations belonging to CITES banned the trade in elephant ivory in 1989.

What is a cloudburst?

A cloudburst is a downpour of unusually heavy rain. A fall of 2 inches of rain in 12 minutes is heavy. A fall of 1.5 inches in one minute, reported on the West Indian island of Guadeloupe in 1970, is exceptional.

WHERE?

Where is the international date line?

Halfway around the world from the Greenwich meridian (0° longitude) is the 180th meridian. Along most of it runs the international date line, where every new calendar day begins. People living east of the line are almost a day behind those who live just west of it.

Where is the lowest point in Africa?

Lake Assal in Djibouti, a small country in eastern Africa, is 500 feet below sea level and is the lowest point in Africa.

Where is Kashmir?

Kashmir is a spectacularly beautiful region of valleys and rivers. It is between the Karakoram mountains and the western Himalayas and is disputed by India and Pakistan.

Where does most of our oil come from?

Most of the petroleum we use comes from the Middle East, which has more than 60 percent of the world's oil. Saudi Arabia has about one-fifth of the world's oil reserves (the amount left in the ground that can be used).

Where are the jet streams?

These are fast-moving currents of air that are found at a height of between 6 and 9 miles in the atmosphere.

Where would you find contours?

You would find them on a map. Contours are lines drawn on a map joining places that are the same height above sea level.

Where is Mindanao?

In the Philippines, a large group of islands in Southeast Asia. It is the second largest island in the country. Manila, the capital of the Philippines, is on the largest island, Luzon.

Where are the horse latitudes?

These are atmospheric zones of high pressure about 30° north and south of the equator, marked by calms and variable light winds.

Where are the Roaring Forties?

South of 40° south latitude, there are prevailing (steady) northwest to westerly winds that blow fiercely all the time. Sailors entering this ocean region named it the Roaring Forties.

Where are the Cairngorms?

These are the highest mountains in the British Isles, in northwest Scotland. The name comes from one of the peaks, Cairn Gorm, which is 4,109 feet high.

Where are the antipodes?

Two places exactly opposite each other on the Earth's surface are antipodes. British people sometimes call Australia and New Zealand the Antipodes because these lands are on the far side of the world from Britain. However, it is not possible to tunnel through the Earth to link Britain and Australia!

Where is the Gulf of Bothnia?

The Gulf of Bothnia may be found in the Baltic Sea. On its shores are Sweden and Finland. The Gulf of Bothnia is often frozen in winter, and there are many small islands.

Where is Monument Valley?

Monument Valley is in Utah. Reddish sandstone rocks rise up like towers and castles from the surrounding land. These rocks are hundreds of millions of years old. The rocks that once surrounded the "monuments" have been worn away by erosion and weathering.

Where are the polar circles?

The Arctic and Antarctic circles are imaginary lines bordering the polar regions. The Arctic Circle is at 66° 32′ north latitude; the Antarctic Circle is at 66° 32′ south latitude.

Where do meteoroids come from?

Some meteoroids are fragments of material left over after the planets formed which have orbited the Sun ever since like tiny planets. Others are particles thrown out from comets.

Where are the Faeroe Islands?

Halfway between the Shetland Islands and Iceland, in the North Atlantic are the Faeroe Islands. There are 18 rocky and windswept islands, belonging to Denmark, and about 40,000 people live on them.

Where is Mount Cook?

This peak, 12,349 feet high, is the highest mountain in New Zealand.

Where is the Nullarbor Plain?

The Nullarbor is a vast, dry desert area in southern Australia. Across it runs the world's longest straight railway track.

Where do the Afars and Issas live?

They live in Djibouti, a small, hot and dry republic in eastern Africa that borders the Red Sea. Before it became independent in 1977, it was a French colony called the Territory of the Afars and Issas after the two ethnic groups that make up most of the population.

Where is the Gulf of Guinea?

This Gulf is off West Africa. Countries that have coastlines on the Gulf of Guinea include Nigeria, Benin, Togo, and Ghana.

Where was Atlantis?

Atlantis, according to legend, was a lost island beneath the sea. In about 1470 B.C. a volcano exploded on the island of Thera (Santorini) in the Aegean Sea. It caused a huge wave that struck Crete, possibly destroying its Minoan civilization. This may have given rise to the legend of Atlantis.

Where do the Merina people live?

The Merina live on Madagascar, an island off the east coast of Africa.

Where are fossil remains dug out of a tar pit?

The La Brea tar pits in Los Angeles are a rich source of Ice Age fossils. In the pits are the bones of saber-toothed cats, wolves, camels, giant ground sloths, and other extinct animals. The animals came to drink in the pool above the tar pit, became trapped in the boggy tar and died. Their skeletons were well preserved.

Where do the White and Blue Nile join?

The White and Blue Nile join at Khartoum, the capital of the Sudan. The White Nile flows north from Uganda and the Blue Nile flows northwest from Ethiopia. The Nile then flows north through Egypt to the Mediterranean Sea.

Where is North America's most fertile farming area?

North America's most fertile farmlands lie in the eastern part of the Interior Plains, a flat and low-lying region that covers much of central Canada and the Midwest United States.

Where does the ghibli blow?

The ghibli blows across the Fezzan, a desert region of Libya in North Africa. The ghibli is a fierce desert wind.

Where is Antarctica's highest point?

The Vinson Massif in western Antarctica is 16,864 feet above sea level.

Where is the Bass Strait?

The Bass Strait is between Australia and Tasmania. It is named after the British navigator George Bass who discovered the strait in 1798.

Where is the Northwest Passage?

This is a route through the icy seas of the Arctic, impassable for most of the year. Many European sailors died seeking a sea route through the Arctic to Asia. Not until the 1900s was the Northwest Passage conquered. The Arctic ice is too thick for it ever to become a commercial sea route.

Where can you see the Natural Bridge, Natural Tunnel, and Natural Chimneys?

These natural rock landmarks may be seen in the state of Virginia. Water has cut away soft rock to make a bridge and a tunnel big enough for a railway to be built through it. The Natural Chimneys are seven rock towers more than 100 feet high.

Where do ferns usually grow?

These plants prefer moist, shady places. They are thickest in tropical forests, carpeting the floor and growing on tree trunks.

Where is the Banda Sea?

This is one of several small seas in which lie the thousands of islands of Indonesia. Other seas in what is really part of the Pacific Ocean are the Java Sea, the Flores Sea, and the Arafura Sea.

Where would you find podsol?

Podsol is a kind of soil found in cold northern lands. It is greyish white and not particularly fertile because most of the minerals have been washed out.

Where are the Lipari Islands?

There is a group of islands in the Tyrrhenian Sea off the coast of Italy. The chief island Lipari was, in Greek myth, where Aeolus kept the winds confined in caves.

Where is the biggest mangrove forest?

The Sundarbans is the world's biggest mangrove forest. It stretches almost 2,400 square miles across the coasts of Bangladesh and India. It is a tiger reserve and a major breeding ground for fish.

Where are the finest forests in North America?

Forests cover much of the western mountains of North America. Canada is largely forested and there are also large forests in the east of the United States. The most spectacular forests are those of the Pacific coast. Here grow the tallest trees in the world, the redwoods and giant sequoias, as well as cedar, fir, hemlock, and spruce.

Where is the torrid zone?

Torrid means hot, and the torrid zone is the hottest of the latitudinal zones. It lies between the Tropic of Capricorn and the Tropic of Cancer.

Where was Tethys?

Tethys is the name given to the huge ocean that lay between the prehistoric supercontinents of Gondwanaland (the southern supercontinent) and Laurasia (the northern supercontinent). A small part of this ancient ocean remains as the Mediterranean Sea.

Where is the Ruhr?

This is the main industrial region in western Germany. It is named after a tributary of the Rhine river.

Where is Norrland?

Norrland, the "land of the north," is the northern part of Sweden. It occupies 60 percent of the country.

Where do chamois live?

These goatlike animals live in the mountains of Europe. They are remarkably agile and surefooted, and have a thick underfur for protection against the Alpine snows.

Where is the world's largest bay?

Measured by its shore length, Hudson Bay in Canada is the world's largest bay. Its shoreline measures over 7,000 miles.

Where is the biggest fresh water island on Earth?

The biggest island surrounded by fresh water is in the mouth of the Amazon River in Brazil. It is called Marajo and has an area of 19,000 square miles.

Where does the equator cross Africa?

From west to east the equatorial countries of Africa are Gabon, Congo, Zaire, Uganda, Kenya, and Somalia.

WHEN?

When is a sea not a sea?

Most seas are parts of oceans. The biggest sea is the South China Sea. Some years ago the Malayan Sea held this record. It is the stretch of water between the Indian and South Pacific oceans. But the Malayan Sea is no longer officially a separate sea.

When were the first aerial photo maps made?

The first photos of the ground from the air were taken from a balloon over Paris in 1858. Aerial photos were used during World War I (1914–1918), and during World War II (1939–1945) much of the world was mapped from photos taken from aircraft.

When were Frost Fairs held?

London's River Thames used to be much wider and slower-moving. It froze in very cold winters. When the river froze, Frost Fairs were held on the ice, and the citizens of London flocked onto the frozen Thames to enjoy the fun. The last Frost Fair was held in the winter of 1813–1814.

When did birds first appear on Earth?

Until recently scientists thought that the first bird was *Archaeopteryx*, but two skeletons found in Texas suggest that birds appeared even earlier— about 225 million years ago (75 million years before *Archaeopteryx*). These prehistoric birds were the size of a pheasant, with the rear end of a small dinosaur and the head of a bird.

When was the highest shade temperature recorded?

In 1922 in Libya in North Africa, when a shade temperature of 136°F was recorded.

When did the first ship cross the North Pole?

On August 3, 1958 the U.S. submarine Nautilus crossed the North Pole beneath the Arctic ice.

When was Brazil discovered by Europeans?

The first European sailor to discover Brazil was Pedro Alvarez Cabral, who claimed the new land for Portugal in 1500.

When was Antarctica discovered?

In the 1700s and early 1800s several explorers came close to Antarctica but were halted by the pack ice. In 1840 the American Charles Wilkes followed the coast for 1,400 miles, proving that Antarctica was a vast southern continent.

When was the Mediterranean Sea dry?

About 6 million years ago, when the Mediterranean climate was much warmer and drier than it is now, the Mediterranean Sea was dry.

When did sponges first appear?

From fossil remains it seems that sponges first appeared on Earth in the late Precambrian era, over 600 million years ago.

When were the world's oceans at their greatest extent?

The oceans were largest during the Cretaceous period (65 to 135 million years ago). The continents were already drifting apart. The North Atlantic was opening up, as the so-called Old and New Worlds moved apart.

When did people discover that the Earth is round?

The ancient Greeks studied the shadows of the Earth and Moon during eclipses and discovered that both were round. They thought that the sphere or globe was the perfect shape.

When was the International Geophysical Year?

The International Geophysical Year was 1957–1958. It was a year of scientific exploration, particularly of Antarctica. Dr. Vivian Fuchs of Britain led a British Commonwealth party that made the first land crossing of Antarctica in 98 days.

When does a caracal leap in the air?

The caracal is a lynx, or wildcat, found in Africa and southern Asia. When hunting it catches low-flying birds by leaping into the air.

When was coffee first grown in Brazil?

In the mid 1700s coffee was first grown in Brazil. The natural home of the wild coffee plant is in Ethiopia, in northwest Africa.

When did Japan's most famous volcano last erupt?

Mount Fuji, Japan's sacred mountain and highest peak (12,388 feet), last erupted in 1707.

When did the island of Surtsey appear?

Surtsey is a small volcanic island 12 miles off the coast of Iceland. It rose out of the sea in 1963 as a result of volcanic activity.

When will Europe's population double?

At present Europe has about 685 million people. It will take 115 years for the population to double at the present very low growth rate. The populations of Africa and Asia will double in less than 30 years.

When did a person see the whole world for the first time?

On April 12, 1961 Soviet cosmonaut Yuri Gagarin became the first person to orbit the Earth in a spacecraft.

When was the highest mountain outside Asia climbed?

Cerro Aconagua in Argentina is 22,831 feet and is the highest peak in the Western Hemisphere. It was first climbed in 1897.

When was the voyage of the *Challenger*?

The *Challenger* was the first ship equipped for scientific exploration of the oceans. The *Challenger* was away for three and a half years beginning in 1872. The British scientists on board collected information and specimens of animals and plants.

When was the Earth's population no more than that of the United States today?

This was before A.D. 1000, when it is estimated there were no more than about 300 million people in the world. The population of the United States today is about 250 million.

When did Thomas Huxley collect jellyfish?

In the 1840s, while on a voyage between Australia and New Guinea, Huxley collected jellyfish among other creatures. Huxley, a surgeon in the British Navy, was such a good scientist that the Navy gave him three years to write reports on the jellyfish and other creatures he had collected. Huxley became a famous biologist. He was a friend and supporter of Charles Darwin.

When are polar bear cubs born?

Female polar bears spend much of the Arctic winter hibernating in a snow den. During this time they give birth to their young. The male bears remain awake, hungrily prowling the icy darkness of the polar winter.

When was the Mediterranean Sea linked to the Red Sea?

These seas were linked when the Suez Canal was opened in 1869. The canal was designed by Ferdinand de Lesseps, a French engineer. An earlier canal had existed in the A.D. 600s.

When do hornbills wall themselves in?

These tropical birds nest in hollow trees, and the female is walled in while she is nesting. The male hornbill fills up the entrance with mud, leaving only a small hole through which he passes her food. When the eggs have hatched the mud wall is broken away to release the mother and, when they can fly, the youngsters.

When did Brazil get its name?

The first Europeans to settle Brazil were the Portuguese in the 1500s. They found there trees that had wood the color of a red-hot coal, called *brasa* in Portuguese. They called these trees brazilwoods, and the country took its name from the trees.

When was sugar first grown in America?

Sugar-making may have begun in India 5,000 years ago. Later the Arabs brought sugarcane to Europe. Columbus took sugarcane from Europe to the West Indies in 1493. Sugar became an important crop on plantations in the New World.

When did animals with shells appear on Earth?

The main fossil record begins in the Cambrian period, about 600 million years ago. This is when animals with hard shells began to evolve in the oceans. Before this, animals were soft-bodied, such as jellyfish.

When did the New World get its name?

The Old World was that known to the geographers of ancient times: Europe, Africa, and Asia. When European sailors voyaged to America, in the A.D. 1000s (the Vikings) and the 1400s (Columbus, Cabot, and others), they called it the New World.

When did an earthquake devastate Lisbon?

In 1755 more than 50,000 people in and around the Portuguese capital were killed by an earthquake. The earthquake also produced a freak tidal wave.

When did people first reconstruct extinct animals?

In the early 1800s extinct animals were reconstructed for the first time. One of the first scientists to use fossil bones to work out what long-extinct animals might have looked like was Georges Cuvier (1769–1852). He used his knowledge of anatomy to recreate the appearance of animals such as the giant ground sloths, known only from fossil remains.

When did Charles Darwin journey around the world?

In 1831 Darwin, then a young geologist of 24, set sail from England aboard HMS *Beagle*. The voyage lasted for five years, and what Darwin saw during his visits to South America and the Galapagos Islands helped form his ideas about evolution. When he came home, he wrote a famous book about it.

When did mastodons live?

Mastodons were elephantlike animals that first appeared about 35 million years ago. Much later they gave rise to elephants and mammoths.

When is the vernal equinox?

March 21 is the vernal equinox in the Northern Hemisphere and marks the beginning of spring.

When is pyroclastic rock formed?

Pyroclastic rock is made of particles that are thrown into the air by the force of a volcanic eruption and then settle back on the ground.

When do scientists use carbon 14 dating?

This method is used to find the age of a rock, a fossil, or an object made by people long ago. The process, also known as radiocarbon dating, measures how much radioactivity is left in the object being dated. By comparing this figure with a known scale of radiocarbon decay in trees, scientists can work out the age of objects many thousands of years old.

When was the first oil well drilled?

The first oil well was drilled in 1859, near Titusville in Pennsylvania. The well was drilled by a retired railway employee named Edwin L. Drake, using an old steam engine.

When were the first offshore oil wells sunk?

These were first constructed in the 1890s, off the coast of California. The oil rigs were on jetties built out from the shore.

When did the Maoris reach New Zealand?

The first settlers arrived in canoes from Polynesia in about 1150. Today about 10 percent of New Zealanders are Maoris.

When does the century plant flower?

This plant is common in Mexico, where it is called the maguey, and it flowers about every hundred years. A drink is made from the juice of its leaves.

WHY?

Why are there hailstones in summer?

Snow may form in clouds in summer, but it melts before it reaches the ground and falls as rain. Hailstones are bigger, and the ice in them does not melt as easily. So during a summer thunderstorm, icy hailstones may fall.

Why are the coco-de-mer tree's seeds remarkable?

These trees have the largest seeds, weighing as much as 40 pounds. The coco-de-mer tree grows only in the Seychelles islands in the Indian Ocean.

Why do prairie dogs live in towns?

Prairie dogs (small American rodents) are social animals. They live together in huge colonies called "towns." The biggest prairie dog town covered over 24,000 square miles and was home to 400 million prairie dogs!

Why do farmers grow crops on terraces?

Steps cut into the hillside increase the amount of flat land for farming. In mountainous tropical areas, farmers terrace the slopes to grow rice.

Why do many cities have unclean air?

Few cities now have smoking factory chimneys, which were common before the 1950s. Yet other kinds of air pollution, particularly from car exhausts, make the air unfit to breathe in many cities. Particularly polluted cities are Milan, Beijing, São Paulo, Seoul, and Mexico City. Athens has introduced a traffic-rationing scheme to keep cars off the roads.

Why does the flag of Lebanon have a cedar tree on it?

In biblical times the cedar trees of Lebanon were famous. Their timber was used to build ships for the Phoenician traders. Today, most of the cedars of Lebanon have long been cut, and only a few remain.

Why are cloudy nights in summer warmer than clear nights?

On a cloudy day the clouds reflect much of the sunlight, stopping warmth from reaching the ground. On a cloudy night the clouds trap heat given off by the ground and reflect it downward. This keeps the air warm. On a clear night the heat escapes into space so the night air feels cooler.

Why is Greenland getting thicker?

The ice sheet covering much of Greenland is thicker now than it was ten years ago. This is probably because the world's oceans are warming up. As more water evaporates into the atmosphere, more of it can fall as snow around the North Pole. The snow becomes ice.

Why is the quebracho tree known as the axbreaker?

The quebracho tree grows in Argentina and Paraguay. Its wood is very hard and tough. The name quebracho, from Spanish, means "axbreaker."

Why is the polyphemus moth caterpillar always hungry?

This caterpillar lives in North America. In the first two days of its life it must eat ravenously, consuming 86,000 times its own birth weight!

Why does water flow downhill?

Water, like everything on Earth, is pulled toward the center of the Earth by the force of gravity. We cannot see gravity, but its effects are all around us. Gravity makes water in a river flow downhill. It makes an apple fall to the ground and keeps us from flying off into space.

Why is balsa wood so light?

Balsa wood is one of the lightest woods known. It comes from the balsa tree of Central and South America. It is only one-third of the weight of cork and is so light because as the wood dries its cells fill with air. Native Americans used balsa wood for making rafts. In 1947 the Norwegian scientist Thor Heyerdahl sailed across the Pacific on a balsa raft called the Kon-Tiki.

Why do countries have fishing limits?

Fishing limits protect fish stocks from being exhausted. Many countries now have a 200-mile limit around their coasts. Canada wants to double the limit off Newfoundland to prevent cod and haddock from being wiped out by too many foreign fishing vessels.

Why do some clouds remain sunlit after sunset?

Noctilucent (night-lit) clouds are very high and are probably made of ice crystals or meteoric dust. They are seen in Europe from 15 to 40 nights a year.

Why do animals have territories?

Many animals mark out and defend a territory. They keep out other animals of the same species. This prevents overcrowding and ensures that there is enough food to go around.

Why do some frogs and toads breed with particular haste?

Some amphibians live in places where the rainy season is short and there are no permanent rivers and ponds, just temporary rainpools. When the rains come, the animals must mate and spawn quickly. The eggs must hatch and the tadpoles grow before the pools dry out—in as little as two weeks.

Why is the Red Sea red?

Red-brown seaweed grows thickly on the Red Sea's surface in summer, giving the water a reddish appearance.

Why did Vasco da Gama sail around Africa?

Da Gama (1469–1524) was a Portuguese navigator and the first European to sail to India by way of the Cape of Good Hope (1497–1499).

Why can't turtles lay their eggs in the sea?

Turtle eggs are not waterproof. The female turtle must therefore come ashore and lay her eggs in a hole on the beach. The baby turtle breathes air through the egg's leathery shell.

Why did Cape Horn get this name?

Willem Schouten (about 1567–1625) of Holland sailed around Cape Horn on a voyage to the East Indies. He named the cape after his birthplace.

Why was Elizabeth I, queen of England, interested in geography?

Elizabeth I of England was keenly interested in the daring voyages of her captains, such as Drake and Frobisher. But her main interest was financial, rather than scientific. Often they brought back Spanish treasures. The queen's geographer was John Dee, who wrote accounts of the voyages of exploration.

Why are hedgerows miniature nature reserves?

A hedgerow is a valuable environment for wildlife. A field of crops is not a good home for most animals, but a hedgerow may have a ditch and a grassy bank. This offers shelter and food to small mammals, birds, and insects, as well as wild plants. So farmers who leave hedges, or plant new ones, are helping to conserve wildlife as well as preventing wind and soil erosion of their fields.

Why do some beetles bury dung?

Dung beetles bury balls of animal dung as food for their grubs. They are useful insects because they clear away the waste of other animals, and in burying the dung they help return valuable nitrogen to the soil.

Why does the robber capsid bug take risks?

This insect is a poacher. It runs around the sticky leaves of the rainbow plant of Australia, a plant that catches and feeds on insects. Other insects get stuck but the robber capsid bug feeds on the plant's captives, and yet mysteriously never gets trapped itself.

Why would you need an umbrella on Mount Waialeale?

On Mount Waialeale it rains a lot: this mountain in Hawaii has as many as 350 rainy days a year.

Why do few plants grow around redwoods?

The redwood of the West Coast is one of the world's tallest trees. The redwoods grow so closely together that their branches shut out most of the sunlight, and very few other plants can therefore grow on the forest floor.

Why is Rio de Janeiro so named?

The name of this Brazilian city means "River of January." A Portuguese explorer landed in the great bay in January 1503. He thought the bay must be the mouth of a mighty river which he named Rio de Janeiro. Later the Portuguese founded a settlement by the same name. Today Rio is one of the three largest cities in South America.

Why is the ocelot becoming hard to spot?

The ocelot is a middle-sized spotted cat of the Americas. It has been hunted for its fur, so much so that it is now a rare animal of the wild.

Why do omnivores eat almost anything?

An omnivore is an animal that eats both other animals and plants. Brown bears and rats are omnivorous, as are chimpanzees and many humans.

Why do swimmers avoid sea wasps?

Sea wasps are small but very venomous jellyfish. They drift about in the western Pacific, and their sting can kill.

Why do jumping beans jump?

Jumping beans are the fruits of a spurgelike plant of Central and South America. Caterpillars live inside the bean and feed on it. When the caterpillar moves, the bean jumps.

Why was America not named Columbia?

Christopher Columbus is remembered as the person who "discovered" America in 1492. Yet Columbus received little reward for his voyages of exploration. The New World he discovered was not named after him but after another voyager, Amerigo Vespucci, who first sailed to the Americas in 1497.

Why are rivers so important to farmers?

Rivers are essential for watering farm crops in areas where there is little rainfall. Farmers dig ditches to carry water from the rivers to their fields. River valleys and plains are especially fertile places in which to grow crops. Early civilizations grew in river valleys, where the first farmers settled.

Why might giant vacuum cleaners suck up the seabed in the next century?

The seabed is rich in minerals such as manganese and nickel. The minerals are found as small lumps or nodules. Mining companies may one day suck them up through giant suction hoses suspended from tankers or working platforms on the surface.

Why do deep-sea worms gather at hot springs?

The ocean floor is dark and cold. There is very little food. In some places hot water gushes up, heated by volcanic rocks in the Earth's crust. These hot "oases" are rich in minerals that support bacteria, which in turn feed strange communities of animals —tube worms, mussels, blind crabs, and clams. Some of these animals are scavengers, feeding on waste and dead animals floating down.

Why do some trees have catkins?

The catkin is a hanging spike of flowers. The hazel is one common tree that bears catkins.

Why do some animals have binocular vision?

In many animals the eyes are at the side of the head. In others, such as apes and owls, the eyes are at the front of the head. This gives an overlapping field of view and enables the animal to judge distance more accurately.

Why did people in ancient times admire the aurochs?

The aurochs, now extinct, was a wild ox bigger than a farm cow, with long horns. People hunted the aurochs and later domesticated it, probably by rearing calves. They admired the aurochs' great size and strength.

HOW?

How cold is it when frost forms?

Frost is made of particles of frozen moisture or ice crystals. It forms when the temperature drops below freezing point, 32°F.

How long can a rainbow last?

Most rainbows are seen for only a few minutes. One seen in North Wales in 1979 lasted over three hours. This was very unusual.

How is boulder clay formed?

Boulder clay is a thick clay made from rock and stones crushed by the grinding mass of glaciers and ice sheets.

How did the sierra get their name?

The word sierra is Spanish for "saw." Mountains with jagged peaks are often called sierra, such as the Sierra Nevada in North America and the Sierra Madre in Mexico.

How salty is the sea?

The saltiness (or salinity) of the sea varies according to the amount of salt dissolved in it. Normal sea-water is about 3.5 percent salts.

How hot is a lightning flash?

The hottest lightning flashes occur when there is an immense discharge of energy as the lightning flashes up and down inside thunderclouds. The temperature can reach 50,000°F—hotter than the surface of the Sun, but nothing like the heat of its center.

In how many ways does the Earth move?

The Earth moves once on its own axis every 24 hours; once around the Sun every 365 days; and once with the Sun and the other planets, spiraling around within the Milky Way, every 250 million years or so.

How cold is the world's coldest inhabited place?

Oymyakon in Siberia holds the record for the coldest place outside Antarctica. In the 1930s a winter temperature of −90°F was measured at Oymyakon, which makes it the world's coldest permanently inhabited place.

How likely are you to be hit by a meteorite?

There is very little risk of being hit by a meteorite. Only very large meteorites hit the Earth. Most burn up in the atmosphere. Only 150 or so hit the ground each year.

How is a caldera formed?

A caldera is a very large volcanic crater. It forms when a number of smaller craters either explode, collapse, or merge into one.

How can we make artificial snow?

To ski, people need snow. If not enough snow falls in the mountains, it is possible to cover the ski slopes with artificial snow. Snow-making machines mix compressed air and water and squirt them into the air in a high-pressure jet. Provided the air is cold enough (25°F or less), the mixture freezes and falls as snow.

How did Nicaragua get its name?

The original inhabitants of Central America were Indians. The first Europeans to move in were the Spaniards in the 1500s. They met an Indian tribe and its chief, who both had the same name—Nicarao. So the Spaniards called the new country Nicaragua.

How long is an epoch?

An epoch is a measurement of geological time. Geologists divide the Earth's history into eras, periods, and epochs. Epochs are the shortest of these time spans. We live in the Holocene epoch which started about 10,000 years ago. Before it, the Pleistocene epoch lasted for two million years. Earlier epochs were up to nine times longer. Periods and eras are much longer still.

How many varieties of rice are there?

There are about 120,000 varieties, 60,000 of which are stored at the International Rice Research Institute in the Philippines.

How many active volcanoes are there in Antarctica?

Mount Erebus is the only active volcano on this continent. It rises 12,520 feet above sea level.

How did right whales get their names?

Organized whaling was started by Basque hunters in the Bay of Biscay over 1,000 years ago. They hunted whales that swam slowly and floated when dead. These were the "right" whales (the easiest to catch). Right whales are baleen whales, related to humpback and blue whales.

How many voyages did Columbus make to the Americas?

Columbus visited the Americas four times: in 1492, 1493, 1498, and 1502. On his second and largest voyage he took 17 ships and 1,500 men.

How much of our oil comes from under the sea?

Over 20 percent of the world's oil production comes from under the sea. Some 40 countries have offshore oil.

How are oolites made?

An oolite is an egg-shaped lump of rock. It is built up in layers like an onion, around a central core.

How many giant pandas are there?

The giant panda is one of the world's rarest animals. There are probably not more than 1,000 pandas in China, and about half of them are in nature reserves.

How is alluvial soil made?

Alluvium is gravel, silt, sand, or similar material deposited by a river. Alluvial soils are fertile, and the first civilizations grew from farming communities that settled on alluvial land beside river mouths.

How did the Jurassic period get its name?

The Jurassic is named after the Jura Mountains in Switzerland. The Jurassic period began about 190 million years ago and ended about 136 million years ago. There were then just two large continents: Laurasia and Gondwanaland.

How long is Europe's second longest river?

Europe's longest river, the Volga, is 2,194 miles long. Europe's next longest river is the Danube which is 1,777 miles long.

How fast does lightning travel?

Lightning travels faster on its "return stroke," after it hits the ground. It reaches a speed of 84,000 miles per second—nearly half the speed of light.

How many islands are there in the Philippines?

There are about 7,000 islands, but only 10 percent have people living on them. The largest islands are Luzon and Mindanao.

How high is France's highest mountain?

Mont Blanc (meaning "white mountain") is the highest mountain in France. It rises to 15,780 feet on the Italian border.

How is the Red Sea getting wider?

New rock is being added to the Earth's crust in the center of the Red Sea, pushing Arabia northeastward. If this continues, the Persian Gulf will close up and become a fold mountain range.

How do salmon find their way home?

Salmon are fish that are born in a river, swim down to the sea, and then after a year or so return to the same river to breed. A salmon probably uses the Sun to navigate across the open sea. It relies on smell at the river mouth to make sure it has the right river. Its journey upstream is difficult, since the fish has to swim against the river's flow, even leaping up waterfalls to reach its birthplace. There it mates, lays its eggs, and dies.

How small is Europe's smallest country?

The Vatican City in Rome covers 0.18 square miles. Monaco is a bit larger—0.75 square miles, and San Marino is roomy by comparison—24 square miles.

How was the Roman town of Pompeii destroyed?

In A.D. 79 the volcano Mount Vesuvius erupted. The town of Pompeii was buried by volcanic ash. Many of its citizens died trying to escape. The town was preserved as the hot ash cooled and solidified, and its ruins have been uncovered by archaeologists to reveal streets and houses.

How many time zones are there in America?

The United States and Canada are so wide that they cover six standard time zones, with an hour's difference between each one.

How long is the world's "longest" country?

The north-south extent of Chile, a long narrow country in South America and the world's longest country, is about 2,600 miles.

How can there be tides in the air?

There are high and low tides in the air just as there are in the oceans, caused by the gravitational pull of the Sun and Moon. Called lunar winds, these air movements are very slow, about 0.05 miles per hour.

How long is the longest earthworm?

The longest earthworm lives in South Africa and is almost 23 feet long. Earthworms help break down humus (decaying matter) in the soil as they burrow their way through the ground.

How many solstices are there?

There are two solstices. The summer solstice is on June 21, when the Sun is overhead at the northern Tropic of Cancer. The winter solstice is on December 21, when the Sun is overhead at the southern Tropic of Capricorn.

How big is the biggest mollusk?

The record-breaking mollusk is the giant squid, which can weigh two tons and measure 50 feet.

How long does it take light to reach us from the Sun?

Light takes about eight minutes to reach the Earth from the Sun. The average distance across the Solar System is 11 light-hours. The nearest star is more than 4 light-years away.

How long is a degree of longitude?

At the equator, each degree of longitude equals 69 miles.

How smooth is the Earth?

From space, the Earth looks like a small ball. In fact, its surface is wrinkled, folded, and crumpled by mountains, volcanoes, and glaciers.

How deep is the sea?

The average depth of the ocean is 11,500 feet. The ocean trenches plummet to over 33,000 feet.

How many islands make up the Bahamas?

There are more than 700 islands in the Bahamas, including tiny, rocky islets. One of these islands, San Salvadore, was the first landing place of Christopher Columbus in 1492.

How long have mammals lived on the Earth?

The first mammals appeared during the Triassic period 275 million years ago. They did not become abundant until much later, after the extinction of the dinosaurs about 65 million years ago.

How much water falls as rain?

Each year more than 4 quintillion cubic feet of fresh water falls either as rain or snow. In theory there is enough water for everyone, but this rain and snow falls heavily in some places and hardly at all in others.

Index

Page numbers in *italics* refer to illustrations.

INDEX

ACKNOWLEDGMENTS

The publishers wish to thank the following artists for contributing to this book:

Jonathan Adams; Craig Austin; John Barber; Richard Bonson; Jim Channell; Jeane Colville; Richard Coombs; Peter Dennis; Dave Etchell; Michael Fisher (Garden Studio); Wayne Ford; Chris Forsey; Mark Franklin; Jeremy Gower; Hardlines; Ron Hayward; Ian Jackson; Aziz Khan; Mike Lacey; Adrian Lascom (Garden Studio); Mick Loats; Chris Lyon; Kevin Maddison; Janos Marffy (Middleton Artists Agency); Eva Melhuish; Liz Pepperell; Bernard Robinson; Eric Robson; Nick Shrewing; Swanston Graphics.

The publishers wish to thank the following for kindly supplying photographs for this book:

Page 6 Science Photo Library; 11 Life Science Images; 13 Hulton-Deutch; 14 British Library; 17 Salt Lake Convention Visitors Bureau; 19 Life Science Images; 22 Natural History Museum; 30 South American Pictures; 46 Swift Picture Library; 48 NOAA; 57 South American Pictures; 67 Dennis Gilbert; 98 Hutchison Picture Library; 99 Hutchison Picture Library; 102 Remote Source; 106 Hutchison Picture Library; 108 Helene Rogers/Trip; 115 South American Pictures; 116 South American Pictures; 120 Science Photo Library; 139 Exxon.

All other photographs Zefa.

Picture Research: Su Alexander